# business one : one

Rachel Appleby
John Bradley
Brian Brennan
Jane Hudson

## student's book   intermediate+

OXFORD
UNIVERSITY PRESS

# OXFORD
## UNIVERSITY PRESS

Great Clarendon Street, Oxford OX2 6DP

Oxford University Press is a department of the University of Oxford.
It furthers the University's objective of excellence in research, scholarship,
and education by publishing worldwide in

Oxford  New York

Auckland  Cape Town  Dar es Salaam  Hong Kong  Karachi
Kuala Lumpur  Madrid  Melbourne  Mexico City  Nairobi
New Delhi  Shanghai  Taipei  Toronto

With offices in

Argentina  Austria  Brazil  Chile  Czech Republic  France  Greece
Guatemala  Hungary  Italy  Japan  Poland  Portugal  Singapore
South Korea  Switzerland  Thailand  Turkey  Ukraine  Vietnam

OXFORD and OXFORD ENGLISH are registered trade marks of
Oxford University Press in the UK and in certain other countries

© Oxford University Press 2006

The moral rights of the author have been asserted

Database right Oxford University Press (maker)

First published 2006

2015  2014
10  9

ISBN: 978 0 19 457637 6  (pack)
ISBN: 978 0 19 457635 2  (book)

Printed in China

This book is printed on paper from certified and well-managed sources.

ACKNOWLEDGEMENTS

Business one:one intermediate+ Student's Book was edited by James Greenan.

The Business one:one MultiROM was written by Jane Hudson, Rachel
Appleby, Brian Brennan, Fiona Delaney, David Grant, and Heidi Grant.

Early input on the project was received from Kate Baade, Rose Law, Penny
McLarty, and Susan Tesar.

Many thanks to James Greenan (editor), families and friends, and all our
colleagues and students in Hungary and Spain who have contributed in one
way or another to make this book work.

The Business one:one glossary was produced by Rosalind Combley, with
definitions based on the Oxford Business English Dictionary for learners of
English, © Oxford University Press 2005 and the Oxford Advanced Learner's
Dictionary 7th edition, © Oxford University Press 2005.

*The authors and publishers would like to thank the following people for giving
permission to reproduce interviews:* Ian Middlehurst, Bill Newson, Nicky
Pritchett-Brown, Gemma Sala.

*The authors and publisher are grateful to those who have given permission to reproduce
the following extracts and adaptations of copyright material:* pp 92–93 Extracts from
'Heard the one about the Spanish scratchcard' from *The Observer* 1 September
2002 © Guardian Newspapers Limited 2002. pp 98–99 Extract from 'Credits
and Debits' from *The Renaissance Bazaar: From the Silk Road to Michelangelo* by
Jerry Brotton. Reproduced with kind permission.

*Sources:* p 21 *The Book of Heroic Failures* by Stephen Pile; p 27 http://jn10.co.uk/
stories/funny-but-true-stories.php; p 134 www.extremetech.com

*Art editing by:* Suzanne Williams/Pictureresearch.co.uk

*Illustrations by:* Ian Baker/CartoonStock pp 10, 12, 26, 46, 62, 76, 93; Annie
Boberg/The Organisation pp 24, 36, 50, 74; Mark Duffin pp 41, 107; Andy
Hammond/Illustration pp 4 (man with black eye), 22, 32, 49, 78, 78; Bill
Ledger pp 9, 20, 42, 42, 55, 71; Paul Oakley pp 4 (men talking), 13, 16, 28, 38,
53, 72, 84; Martin Sanders/Mapart p 87; Paul Stroud p 56

*We would also like to thank the following for permission to reproduce the following
photographs:* Action-Plus p 44 (Ascot/Neil Tingle); Alamy pp 14 (call centre/
Fredrik Renander), 20 (Luca DiCecco), 66 (Pat Behnke), 67 (Maurice Joseph);
Corbis p 86 (Yang Liu); Getty Images pp 16 (Romilly Lockyer), 31 (Alberto
Incrocci), 33 (Shannon Fagan), 34 (Spencer Platt), 38 (Greg Pease), 40
(Orlando/ Stringer), 44 (paint-balling /Sean Murphy), 44 (sailing /Southern
Stock), 44 (assault course/Philip Lee Harvey), 51 (Giantstep Inc), 61 (Samuel
Ashfield), 63 (Elizabeth Young), 83 (Sam Diephuis), 88 (Lauren Burke), 101
(Chev Wilkinson), 102 (Jonathan Gregson); Hemisphere Images p 96; The
Kobal Collection p 100 (Lucasfilm/20th Century Fox); Lonely Planet Images
p 90 (Morocco/Wayne Walton); Courtesy of Nokia p 14 (mobile phone);
Courtesy of Nicky Pritchett-Brown p 105; Punchstock pp 4 (woman/Corbis),
11 (Stockbyte), 15 (Image Source), 19 (BananaStock), 22 & 25 (image100), 30
(Image Source), 47 (image100), 52 (Stockbyte), 54 (Corbis), 55 (BananaStock),
57 (James Lauritz), 68 (Blend Images), 78 (Spohn Matthieu), 82 (Digital
Vision), 89 (Corbis), 90 (New York/image100), 104 (Stockbyte Platinum); Rex
Features pp 90 (Tokyo/Heikki Saukkomaa), 91 (Ilpo Musto), 95 (Alastair Muir);
Royalty-Free pp 26, 65 & 84 (PhotoDisc); SCALA p 99 (Benozzo Gozzoli (1420-
1497) Palazzo Medici-Riccardi, Florence, Italy); Science Photo Library p 32
(Tony Craddock)

# course syllabus

# How to **ask for something**

**01**

**In this lesson you will learn polite and more direct ways of asking for things.**

## Starter

1 What do you often ask the following people for?

- a boss
- a bank manager
- a customer
- a colleague
- a supplier

2 Talk about the last time you asked these people for these things. Did anything unusual happen?

What did he say about the pay rise?

BOSS

## Expressions

1.1 ○ **1** Listen to the conversation and answer the questions.

1 Who are the speakers?

2 What do they ask for?

3 Who is polite? Who makes demands? Why?

## Speaking

1 Make a suitable request for the following situations. Try to use phrases from Expressions and the Language box. Your teacher will respond to your requests.

1 You ordered twenty colour cartridges for your printer. Unfortunately, you received black cartridges instead. Call the supplier and ask them to correct the order.

2 You ask your boss if you can have the morning off next Friday because you need to sign some papers at the bank.

3 You ask for a return train ticket to Oxford at the ticket office.

4 Your colleague keeps forgetting to finish the report you have both been working on. It needs to be sent to head office today. You call him to help him remember.

1.2 ○ **2** Listen to four conversations role-playing situations 1–4. Compare them to your requests.

**Hint**

Be careful with pronunciation when making requests:

Polite requests are made with high intonation (the voice goes up).

Demanding requests are made with lower intonation (the voice goes down).

**2** Look at the extracts from the conversation. Complete them with the phrases used for asking for something.

1 Hello. I _____ speak to Susan Crawley, please.

2 Would you _____ me a duplicate?

3 Now we'd _____ pay for the computers.

4 Do you _____ wait until next month?

5 We _____ pay before the end of June.

6 If we _____ payment by then, _____ we'll have to send someone round to pick up the computers.

**3** Look at the extracts in **2** again. Mark them polite (P) or demanding (D). Then explain your decision to your teacher.

## Writing

**1** You have received the following note from your boss. Write an email to the travel agency requesting information for his trip.

> Hi
>
> I need some info from El Corte Inglés Travel Agency. I'm going to Milan Conference 10–12 Feb. Need to know:
>
> - flights
> - cost of tickets
> - arrival time back here in Madrid.
>
> Would you mind finding out for me?
> Thanks
> Jack

## Look

Look again at listening script 1.1 and 1.2 on page 111. Find other examples of these structures.

## Language box

We can use *would like* in different ways to ask people for something:

I'd like a cup of tea, please.

I'd like to phone home, if you don't mind.

We'd like you to send the cheque today.

The following verbs can also use the verb + object + infinitive pattern.

> advise   ask   expect   need
> remind   tell   warn

We would ask you to pay in full by 1st May.

We have warned them to pay promptly.

Remember to use *-ing* after *Would you mind*:

**Would you mind** opening the window?

Not   ~~Would you mind to open the window?~~

## Lesson record

| 3 new words from this lesson | 3 useful phrases from this lesson |
|---|---|
| 1 .................... | 1 ........................ |
| 2 .................... | 2 ........................ |
| 3 .................... | 3 ........................ |

Things to remember

..................................................................

..................................................................

..................................................................

..................................................................

..................................................................

..................................................................

..................................................................

# How to **make a suggestion**

## In this lesson you will practise different ways to put forward ideas.

### Starter

1 Is there any truth in these humorous quotes?

2 How important is the role of the consultant in business?

3 Would you like to be a consultant?

> "Consultants are people who borrow your watch and tell you what time it is, and then walk off with the watch."
>
> Robert Townsend
>
> source: http://www.brainyquote.com/quotes/quotes/r/roberttown165640.html

> "All too many consultants, when asked, "What is two and two?" respond, "What do you have in mind?""
>
> Norman R. Augustine
>
> source: http://www.brainyquote.com/quotes/quotes/n/normanrau204561.html

### Expressions

1 Bruston Bicycles and Cycling Accessories Ltd is in trouble. Sales are 15% down on last year. It is losing clients. Three of its best sales people have left the company in the last two months. To find out what's going wrong Bright Ideas Ltd, a business consulting group, visited the company a few days ago and made the notes below.

Read the notes and then discuss the different problems with your teacher. In your opinion, which are the three most important issues, and why?

#### BRIGHT ideas

1 Sales and Production - only monthly meetings
2 staff not given enough information
3 products old-fashioned - design manager left a year ago - not replaced
4 company doesn't use Internet at all
5 name of company!
6 sales manager obviously overworked - covers national and export sales - no assistant
7 John Bruston - managing director - 79 years old, son of founder
8 reputation for top quality, but delays of up to a month in deliveries

### Speaking

1 Your friend comes to you with the following problems. Make two suggestions in each case. Use as many different expressions as you can.

> "I frequently travel to Germany but I don't speak a word of the language."

> "I just feel I'm going nowhere in my job."

> "I often forget things like meetings and phone numbers."

> "My car's always breaking down!"

> "I feel so tired and overworked."

### Writing

1 You are not happy with the following five things. Tell your teacher why you are not happy and what you would change if you could. Make two different suggestions or proposals about:

1 the organization of your classes (days, time, etc.)

2 the place where you work

3 the work timetable or calendar that you have

4 the TV programmes in the country where you live

5 the traffic and / or parking problems in the city where you live.

2 Explain the reasons behind your proposals. Find out if your teacher agrees with you. Choose one of the topics and write an email to an appropriate person, containing your proposals.

**Hint**

You can **make** or **put forward a suggestion / proposal** to somebody.

**2.1**

**2** Listen to the presentation that one consultant from Bright Ideas gives to the management of Bruston. He mentions four of the problem areas. Which ones?

**3** Now listen again. This time complete the spaces with the words the man uses to make his proposals.

1 First of all, we _____ a change to the company's name.

2 We _____ to a more international name.

3 Secondly, we'd like to _____ new sales staff.

4 We _____ three new assistant staff – people with languages and experience.

5 Our third _____ the possible use of the Internet as a marketing tool for your company.

6 Finally, we _____ serious and immediate measures to reorganize the production side of the company.

**2.2**

**4** The consultant and the sales manager go to lunch. Listen to their conversation. What problems does the consultant mention?

**5** The consultant uses the following expressions. Listen again and complete the sentences below with his suggestions.

1 Have you _____ the name?

2 You've got big problems there. _____ making meetings more frequent?

3 And, well, I don't really know how _____, but …

4 How _____ somebody younger to do his job?

5 Let's _____ , some of your products look really old. _____ you employed a new designer?

## Language box

Two verbs that are often used for making suggestions or proposals are *suggest* and *recommend.* Look at the following examples:

We recommend changing the dates.

We recommend that you change the name.

We suggest using the Internet.

We suggest that you use the Internet.

**Other expressions:**

How about changing your job?

Have you considered changing your job?

What if you change / changed your job?

We'd like to propose that you invest €9,000.

## Look

Look again at listening scripts 2.1 and 2.2 on page 111. Find all the examples of suggestions.

## Lesson record

| 3 new words from this lesson | 3 useful phrases from this lesson |
|---|---|
| **1** .................... | **1** ........................................ |
| **2** .................... | **2** ........................................ |
| **3** .................... | **3** ........................................ |

Things to remember

..................................................................

..................................................................

..................................................................

..................................................................

..................................................................

..................................................................

# How to **react to suggestions**

## 03

**In this lesson you will learn ways of accepting or rejecting suggestions.**

### Starter

1 Do you have any colleagues with the following habits?

- They make personal phone calls in a loud voice.
- They arrive late and leave early.
- They never return items they borrow.
- They use bad language all the time.
- Their only subject of conversation is their children.
- They waste time and never get anything done.
- They smoke continuously.
- They never pay for drinks or meals when you go out.

2 Which of the habits do you find most annoying?

3 How could you deal with these colleagues?

### Expressions

3.1 ○ 1 Listen to four situations where someone is making a suggestion. Answer the following questions for dialogues 1–4 by filling in the columns in the table.

1 What is the annoying habit?
2 What is the suggestion?
3 Is the suggestion accepted (✓) or rejected (✗)?

| | habit | suggestion | ✓ / ✗ |
|---|---|---|---|
| 1 | | | |
| 2 | | | |
| 3 | | | |
| 4 | | | |

### Writing

1 Read the following email and suggest ways the supervisor could deal with the problems in the department. Role-play a conversation to follow the email, with you as Charlie and your teacher as Sam.

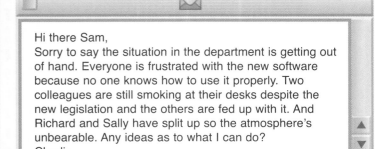

Hi there Sam,
Sorry to say the situation in the department is getting out of hand. Everyone is frustrated with the new software because no one knows how to use it properly. Two colleagues are still smoking at their desks despite the new legislation and the others are fed up with it. And Richard and Sally have split up so the atmosphere's unbearable. Any ideas as to what I can do?
Charlie

2 Reply to the email with your own ideas.

### Language box

When we react to a suggestion, we often suggest specific action, or propose a possible alternative for action. Look at the expressions used to react to the following suggestion:

> Everyone in the office seems a bit down. Why don't we all go out together?
>
> That's a good idea ...
>
> ... We could have dinner and then go out dancing.
>
> ... Let's start planning it right now.
>
> ... It would be even better if the company paid for a party!
>
> ... Shall we put up a poster?

**2** Look at the extracts from the four conversations below. Complete them with the useful phrases for reacting to suggestions.

1 No, _____ do that.
  It would be really embarrassing.

2 No, I'm _____ that's
  such a good idea.
  She is the boss _____ !

3 OK, that _____ ,
  I suppose.

4 What _____ ! I'll do
  that next time he calls.

## Speaking

**3.2 ○ 1** Listen to conversations 1–4. Match each one with a picture a–d below.

**2** Your teacher will suggest ways to deal with the situations. Respond in an appropriate way.

## Look

Look again at conversations 1–4 in listening script 3.2 on pages 111–112. Find more expressions used to react to suggestions.

---

*Shall* is used with *we* and *I*, especially in British English. It is often used to make suggestions along with *let's.*

  Shall we leave now?

  Yes, let's / let's go.

When we reject a suggestion, we normally give a reason:

  Mm, I'm not so sure about that ...

  ... It might make things worse.

  ... I think people would prefer a bonus to a
  night out.

---

## Lesson record

| 3 new words from this lesson | 3 useful phrases from this lesson |
|---|---|
| 1 .................... | 1 .................................... |
| 2 .................... | 2 .................................... |
| 3 .................... | 3 .................................... |

Things to remember

..................................................................

..................................................................

..................................................................

..................................................................

..................................................................

..................................................................

# How to **praise**

**04**

**In this lesson you will learn useful language for giving positive feedback to colleagues.**

## Starter

1   In what circumstances do you praise colleagues at work?

2   Do you find giving praise or receiving praise more difficult? Why?

" I'M SO, SO, SO, SO PROUD OF YOU !! "

## Expressions

4.1 ○ **1**   Listen to three situations where someone is giving praise.

1   In each dialogue 1–3, what did someone do well?

2   What has happened as a result?

| | what they did well | result |
|---|---|---|
| **1** | | |
| **2** | | |
| **3** | | |

## Speaking

1   Role-play the following situations to practise giving praise. Your teacher will play the person being praised. Before you begin, decide how you will introduce the topic, and what specific aspect(s) you will praise.

1   Boss to employee – praise for a report.

2   Boss to employee – praise on winning a large new contract.

3   Colleague to colleague – praise for the new company website.

4.2 ○ **2**   Now listen to two conversations role-playing the first two situations above. Compare them with your version.

## Language box

In the conversations, different words are used to make adjectives stronger or weaker. Here is how you can change the strength of the adjective *good*:

| | |
|---|---|
| **WEAKER** | pretty / fairly / **quite** good |
| | good |
| ↓ | pretty / fairly / quite **good** |
| | really / very good |
| **STRONGER** | extremely good |

Note that if you stress *pretty / fairly / quite*, it makes the adjective weaker. If you stress the adjective after *pretty / fairly / quite*, it makes it stronger.

**Hint**

When praising, it's usual to introduce what you say with a more general comment:
**I just wanted to mention …**
**I'd just like to say …**
**By the way, …**
**Oh, have you got a minute?**

**2** Look at the extracts from the three conversations below. Complete them with the useful phrases for giving praise from listening script 4.1. Then listen again and check your answers.

1 I'd just like to say I'm _____ how successful our stand was …

2 Jane, you _____ to get such a good location.

3 Well _____, Jane.

4 I want to tell you _____ your presentation yesterday. You did a _____ .

5 I really _____ included the customer stories.

6 Anyway, they love it – you _____ very well.

## Writing

**1** One of your colleagues has just returned from an international conference, where they represented your company. You hear that their presentation went very well. As you are working from home, you decide to drop them an email to congratulate them.

**2** You are the boss of a small retail store. A new member of staff noticed that somebody was regularly stealing from you, and by reporting it to you has saved you a lot of money. Write a letter to the member of staff, praising them and telling them the results of their action.

You can also replace the adjective with a stronger one:

extremely good < fantastic / excellent < absolutely excellent

But you have to be careful using strong adjectives like *excellent*, *fantastic*, *amazing*, *wonderful*, etc. You cannot use *very* with these words. You must use *really* or *absolutely*.

That was absolutely brilliant.

That was a really fantastic presentation.

Not ~~It was a very fantastic performance.~~

## Look

Look again at conversations 1–3 in listening script 4.1 on page 112. Find examples of *pretty / fairly / quite* and listen again. In each case, is it making the adjective weaker or stronger?

**Lesson record**

| 3 new words from this lesson | 3 useful phrases from this lesson |
|---|---|
| 1 .................... | 1 ................................. |
| 2 .................... | 2 ................................. |
| 3 .................... | 3 ................................. |

Things to remember

................................................................
................................................................
................................................................
................................................................
................................................................
................................................................

# How to **criticize**

## 05

**In this lesson you will learn useful language for giving negative feedback to colleagues.**

### Starter

5.1 ○ **1** Listen to a short conversation. A manager is giving feedback to a colleague, but she doesn't do it very well. What problem is she dealing with, and what's wrong with her approach? How could you improve it?

5.2 ○ **2** Now listen to the same situation, but done more effectively. How is the manager's approach different?

**3** What is your approach for giving negative feedback to colleagues?

IAN BAKER.

### Expressions

5.3 ○ **1** Listen to two short dialogues. For each, decide who the people are, and what is being criticized.

| who is speaking? | what is being criticized? |
|---|---|
| 1 | |
| 2 | |

**2** Now listen again to the two short dialogues. Complete the spaces with the words used in the recording.

1 Well, _____ I'm quite busy at the moment.

2 The thing is, _____ I can't really stay late at work because of the children.

3 I'd be _____ fix times when you need to discuss work with me.

4 OK. Well. _____ the report you sent.

### Speaking

**1** Imagine you have to deal with the following situations, in which you have to give feedback. Plan what you will say. Role-play the situations with your teacher.

1 You share an office with a colleague who often goes out, without telling you for how long. When clients phone, you are unable to tell them when to call back. What suggestions can you give your colleague?

2 One of your staff, who often visits clients, insists on wearing jeans at work, despite the office dress code which states 'no jeans'. You feel it is necessary to discuss it formally with the staff member.

5.4 ○ **2** Now listen to a conversation role-playing the second conversation in **1** above. Compare it to your version.

### Language box

To describe a difference between two things, we can use *not as ... as ...* Look at the following example:

   We're not as busy as last month.

For smaller differences, use *not quite as ...* For bigger differences, use *not nearly as ...,* or *nothing like as ...* :

   The design isn't quite as attractive as we'd hoped.

   These pictures aren't nearly as good as the last ones.

   Your work is nothing like as good as it was.

dealing with people

## Hint

When criticizing, it is a good idea to use a lead-in phrase such as **'I'm afraid …'**, **'Sorry, but …'**, **'Well actually …'**, and a 'softener' such as **'not very'**, **'a bit'**, **'rather'**, etc.:
**I'm afraid we found your report a bit vague.**

5 Well, maybe I _____
one or two things.

6 Perhaps I _____ you
one of Mike's reports.

7 Do you _____ try
next time?

## Writing

1 Your boss was rude to you in front of a client, which was very embarrassing. This was not the first time. Write an email to your boss, criticizing their behaviour.

2 You have received the formal complaint below. Write an email to all staff explaining the situation, and asking them to wash their own cups up.

## Memo

From: Cleaning
To: Manager of Sales department

We've had problems recently with the kitchen in your department. Cups are left in the sink, food containers are left lying around and no one does the washing-up. It's not our job in the cleaning department to do the washing-up in the kitchen, so please ask your staff to see to this.

Thank you.

---

You can also use *(not) so* … and *(not) such* … to criticize the actual situation:

Please try not to take so long over lunch again.

We won't make the deadline if we work so slowly.

Please don't use such bad language!

I shouldn't have sent such an angry email.

## Look

Look again at the conversations in listening scripts 5.1–5.4 on pages 112–113. Find more examples of these structures.

## Lesson record

| 3 new words from this lesson | 3 useful phrases from this lesson |
|---|---|
| **1** .................... | **1** ................................... |
| **2** .................... | **2** ................................... |
| **3** .................... | **3** ................................... |

Things to remember

.................................................................
.................................................................
.................................................................
.................................................................
.................................................................
.................................................................

# How to **show how to do something**

## 06

## In this lesson you will practise explaining things.

### Starter

1   Have you learnt to do anything new recently? Can you explain it to your teacher?

2   If you have a mobile phone with you, explain to your teacher how to use some of the features: text messaging, taking photos, games, etc.

3   Have you ever had to phone a call centre for help? What about?

### Expressions

6.1 ○ **1**   Rajiv manages a call centre in India. He's explaining the job to Davina, a new worker. Listen to Rajiv's instructions to Davina. What are the main things she needs to remember? Make notes.

6.2 ○ **2**   Listen to Rajiv and Davina take two calls. Mark each sentence true (T) or false (F).

1   The first caller's computer is new. _____

2   Having the caller's password helps Rajiv to solve his problem. _____

3   The second caller can't connect to the Internet. _____

4   Davina tells him there's no immediate solution. _____

### Speaking

1   Explain to your teacher how to follow a work process that you have to do, or how to use a machine in your office.

2   Your teacher will now explain to you how to do something. You can ask questions to check.

### Language box

We use the zero conditional to describe something that always happens in certain conditions. This is very common when we're showing someone how to do something.

> **If you press** this button, **it records** the conversation.

> **This light goes on if you have** another call waiting.

Notice that the two parts of the sentence can come in any order.

There are several variations of this structure:

> **When you click** on this icon, a new window pops up.

> **As soon as this light comes** on, you're connected to the caller.

> You can change the information **as long as you check** with me first.

**dealing with people**

**Hint**

To check that someone has understood, you can ask:

**Is that clear?**

**Any questions?**

Or say:

**I hope that's clear.**

**3** Look at the extracts from the conversations below. Complete them with the phrases used for giving instructions. Then listen again to recordings 6.1 and 6.2 and check your answers.

1 Rajiv: And how is the training going?

Davina: So _____ .

2 Now, one other thing: we have a lot of calls, so _____ aren't any longer than they need to be.

3 Be patient with the caller but _____ the time.

4 You're connected and you should greet the caller. Have _____ ?

5 Sometimes very easy solutions like that are the hardest to find. So, _____ them.

6 Be _____ say 'good morning'.

## Writing

**1** You're attending a meeting in another country for a week. Leave a junior colleague instructions about how to complete a small project that is in progress at the moment.

**2** A friend is going to be staying in your house for a few days, but you'll be at work. Leave instructions for them so that they can work the CD player, TV, DVD / video, or a home computer to check email.

The copier doesn't work **until you key** in your code.

You don't need to re-start the machine **unless this message appears.**

You can also use an imperative:

Just **watch** me and **ask** any questions.

**Be** careful not to tell anyone your password.

## Look

Look at listening scripts 6.1 and 6.2 on page 113. Find more examples of the zero conditional.

**Lesson record**

| 3 new words from this lesson | 3 useful phrases from this lesson |
|---|---|
| **1** .................... | **1** ........................................ |
| **2** .................... | **2** ........................................ |
| **3** .................... | **3** ........................................ |

Things to remember

......................................................................

......................................................................

......................................................................

......................................................................

......................................................................

......................................................................

......................................................................

# How to **delegate**

In this lesson you will learn expressions to use when you are giving people different jobs to do.

## Starter

1   To what extent do you agree with these comments about delegation?

'When you delegate work, you need to check all the time that the job is being done right.'

'You can only ask people to help you if you are their boss.'

'If possible, it's best to do a job yourself rather than delegate.'

'When you delegate, tell the person to work as quickly as possible, to leave yourself a lot of time to check their work at the end.'

'Just tell the person what they need to do, not the small details.'

'People enjoy having work delegated to them.'

## Expressions

7.1 ○ **1**   David Jackson is a sales manager. He broke his leg in a skiing accident last week and will be off work for several weeks. He phones his boss, Arthur Little, to talk about work. Complete the first column with the different jobs he mentions.

|   | job | person |
|---|-----|--------|
| 1 |     |        |
| 2 |     |        |
| 3 |     |        |
| 4 |     |        |
| 5 |     |        |

7.2 ○ **2**   Arthur organizes a meeting to announce the changes. In the second column above, write the name of the person who will be doing each job.

## Speaking

1   Spend a few minutes brainstorming:

- a list of all the people, companies, departments, etc. that give work to you to do
- a list of all the people, companies, departments, etc. that you give work to.

Include both your job and your life outside work (e.g. professional services, family, friends).

2   Talk your teacher through the lists, giving details about the work involved. Try to use language from the unit.

dealing with people

## Hint

If you think something is true, but you need to check it, you can use a negative question:
**Won't you be back at work by then?**

The two possible replies are:

**Yes** (= I will be back at work)
**No** (= I won't be back at work).

**3** Look at the extracts from the meeting below. Complete them with the phrases that Arthur uses for delegating tasks. Then listen to recording 7.2 again and check your answers.

1 Do you think you _____ , Rob?

2 And Susan, I'd like you _____ the job interviews ...

3 I need _____ brochures for the trade fair.

4 Could I _____ , Monica?

5 No, that's not necessary. We can _____ David.

7.3 ○ **4** Rob and Susan go for a coffee after the meeting with Arthur. Listen to their conversation. How does Rob feel about the meeting? Why?

## Writing

**1** Imagine that Arthur Little has no time for the meeting with his team. Write an informal memo to Monica passing on his instructions to her. Use the following memo to Rob as an example. Try to use the language from this unit in your memo.

---

## Memo

Subject: Visit to Samson Ltd

From: Arthur Little
To: Rob Harris

As you know, David is going to be off work for several weeks. In his absence I would like you to look after his client, Samson Ltd. David was going to visit them on the 17th. Please phone them to confirm the appointment, and let them know that you are looking after the contract until David is back.

Arthur Little
General Manager

---

## Look

Look again at listening scripts 7.1–7.2, on pages 113–114. Find examples of these structures.

## Language box

When delegating work, you can use the following expressions with the verbs *ask* and *get*:

I'm going to ask Peter to phone you.
I'll ask Peter if he can phone you.
I'll get Peter to phone you.

You can also use *have*. Note that *to* is not used:

I'll have Peter phone you.

When using a professional service to do a piece of work, you can use *get / have* something *done*:

I need to get my car serviced.
We should have the office redecorated.

## Lesson record

| 3 new words from this lesson | 3 useful phrases from this lesson |
|---|---|
| 1 .................... | 1 ............................ |
| 2 .................... | 2 ............................ |
| 3 .................... | 3 ............................ |

Things to remember

..............................................................
..............................................................
..............................................................
..............................................................
..............................................................
..............................................................

# How to **compromise**

## 08

**In this lesson you will learn how to negotiate a solution to a problem.**

## Starter

1  Do you often have to reach compromises in your job? Think of an occasion when you solved a disagreement or problem by compromising.

2  It can be difficult to combine work with family life. What kinds of compromises do employees and their employers have to reach?

> as parts or members that form something
>
> **compromise** /ˈkɒmprəmaɪz/ when people are arguing, they make an agreement called a compromise by giving up part of what they want
>
> **compulsion** /kəmˈpʌlʃn/ strong force or pressure making someone do something they do not want to

## Expressions

**8.1○ 1**  Derek is the owner of a chain of Turkish restaurants in Ireland. The manager of one of the restaurants is a Turkish woman called Ayse. She wants to talk to Derek about something important. Read this summary of the first part of the dialogue. Then listen to the dialogue and correct the text where it is wrong.

Ayse wants to talk to Derek, her boss, because today she's received a letter from her family in Turkey, saying there's a problem at home and they need her to come home for three or four days. Derek seems to understand her problem, and it's a busy week.

**8.2○ 2**  Listen to the second part of the dialogue and underline the part of the sentence in *italics* that is correct.

1  Derek will not agree to Ayse's request because *he cannot manage without her / he feels she is not being honest.*

2  Ayse's main worry is *her duty to her family / money.*

3  They *understand / do not understand* each other's point of view.

**8.3○ 3**  Listen to the third part of the dialogue. What compromise do they reach?

## Speaking

1  Respond to the following problems. Try to use language from the unit.

1  A regular customer says they are having financial problems and cannot pay for the goods or services you have provided. You need the money but do not want to lose a good customer.

2  There is an urgent project at work. Your boss wants you to work extra hours for the next two weeks, including all day Saturday and Sunday. No extra money is available to pay you for this.

**8.4○ 2**  Now listen to a conversation role-playing the first situation above. Compare it to your response.

## Language box

When trying to reach a compromise, we often discuss the effects of possible actions or events on the situation. In order to do this, conditional sentences are often used.

For something that is a small or unreal possibility, or an idea we are against, we use the second conditional.

The *if* part of the second conditional uses the past simple:

> … if I had the chance.
>
> If we bought 10,000 of them, …

The other part, the result, of the sentence uses *would*:

> I would make a lot of changes if I had the chance.
>
> If we bought 10,000 of them, we'd have storage problems.

**Hint**

**Compromise** can be a verb or a noun. If you use the noun, you can **agree on, arrive at, come to, find, make, reach,** or **work out a compromise**.

**4** Look at the extracts from the dialogues. Complete them with the phrases used by Ayse and Derek. Then listen again to all three dialogues and check your answers.

1 I know it's a busy time of year, I do. I _____ your point of view.

2 But put _____ – imagine if it were your family.

3 This is what I suggest. Let's both _____ and I'll phone you tomorrow morning.

4 Right, er ... I've _____ thinking.

5 On the _____, I need someone with your experience and ability with the staff and the customers.

6 So what _____ – if you went in four days' time that would give us time to show the ropes to someone else.

7 Let's _____ then.

## Writing

1 As part of a presentation to new employees, you decide to suggest some 'tips for reaching agreement'. Write four or five tips that you could show as part of the talk.

2 Choose one of the situations in the Speaking section, and write an email to the other person. Use some of the language from the unit, and invent appropriate details.

## Look

Look again at listening scripts 8.1, 8.2, and 8.3 on page 114. Find more examples of the second conditional.

We also use this second conditional for giving advice:

If I were you, I wouldn't accept that offer.

Notice that the two parts of a conditional sentence can be reversed:

If I agreed to those conditions, would it affect my pension?

Would it affect my pension if I agreed to those conditions?

For something that is a bigger possibility or an idea we are in favour of, we use the first conditional (see also unit 13):

If the baby's a girl, we'll call her Helen.

## Lesson record

| 3 new words from this lesson | 3 useful phrases from this lesson |
|---|---|
| 1 ................ | 1 ................................ |
| 2 ................ | 2 ................................ |
| 3 ................ | 3 ................................ |

Things to remember

................................................................

................................................................

................................................................

................................................................

................................................................

................................................................

# How to plan

## Hint

Note that you can **decide sth** or **decide on sth**, with no difference in meaning.
**We need to decide a logo for the brand.**
**We need to decide on a logo for the brand.**

## In this lesson you will learn expressions to use when you are planning future events.

### Starter

1   Does your company have any of the following plans for the future? Tell your teacher about them.

- to move to a new office
- to enter a new market
- to take part in a conference
- to work with another company on a future venture
- to start a new project
- to win a new contract

2   Have you got any personal plans for the future?

### Expressions

9.1 ○ 1   Listen to two situations where people are making plans. In each situation complete the table in the next column. What are they planning? What three key points do they have to plan?

### Speaking

1   Look at the following situations and for each one think of three key points that have to be planned.

1   Your company is going to make a presentation to another company to try and win a new contract.

2   Your office has been asked to organize the annual group conference.

2   Role-play the first situation with your teacher. Your teacher will start the conversation.

9.2 ○ 3   Listen to a conversation role-playing the same situation. Compare it to your version. Did you choose the same three key points?

4   Now role-play the second situation. This time, you start the conversation.

projects

## Hint

To talk about how we are going to start dealing with a task, we often use the verb **go about something / doing something**:
We can go about this in two ways.
How are we going to go about advertising the launch?

|  | situation 1 | situation 2 |
|---|---|---|
| plan |  |  |
| key points | 1 | 1 |
|  | 2 | 2 |
|  | 3 | 3 |

**2** Look at the extracts from the conversations. Complete them with the phrases used for making plans.

1 So, the first thing we _____ is when we should move.

2 So something _____ is get in touch with a moving company.

3 Who's going to _____ the packing?

4 Have we _____ a name yet, Bob?

5 What we _____ get the advertising campaign organized.

6 I think the _____ is to ask several agencies for samples.

## Writing

**1** Look back to the plans you discussed in the Starter of this unit. Write an email to a person who you are doing the planning with, specifying four or five things that you will need to think about.

**2** Look at the following stories about plans that went wrong.

Mr David Goodall's shoplifting expedition did not go as well as expected. He had hardly entered the department store he was planning to rob when he was caught simultaneously by eight pairs of hands. Unfortunately for him, the shop was holding a convention of store detectives at the time.

On 6th February 1965, Mr Lionel Burleigh opened the Commonwealth Sentinel, Britain's least successful newspaper. Unfortunately, he had to close it again the next day after he received a phone call from the police. 50,000 copies of the newspaper were on the pavement outside the hotel where he was staying, blocking the main road.

source: *The Book of Heroic Failures*, by Stephen Pile.

**3** Using the examples in **2** as a model, write about an experience you have had where your plans went wrong.

## Language box

Use the future perfect for an action that finishes before a certain time in the future.

We will have completed the project before the inspection begins.

We form the future perfect with *will + have + past participle*.

We'll have paid for all the goods before the tax year ends.

We often use the time preposition *by* to mean *before* with the future perfect.

Do you think he'll have finished the course by the end of May?

## Look

Look again at the conversations in listening scripts 9.1 and 9.2 on pages 114–115. Find more examples of the future perfect.

## Lesson record

| 3 new words from this lesson | 3 useful phrases from this lesson |
|---|---|
| 1 .................... | 1 .................... |
| 2 .................... | 2 .................... |
| 3 .................... | 3 .................... |

Things to remember

.................................................................

.................................................................

.................................................................

.................................................................

.................................................................

**10**

## In this lesson you will learn different ways of talking about the progress of a project.

### Starter

1 How do you work out schedules for your projects? How do you monitor progress?

2 Can you remember a project where you ran into time difficulties? Did you solve the time problems or did the project end in disaster?

> We're a little behind schedule....

### Expressions

10.1

1 Listen to a conversation between the general director of an advertising agency and one of the account managers, who is preparing an advertising campaign for Italcafé, a large chain of coffee bars. Tick (✓) the correct column in the chart below.

| job | done | not done |
|---|---|---|
| meet the managing director of Italcafé | | |
| do some market research | | |
| see the ideas of the creative team | | |
| decide which media to use | | |
| arrange a date for the presentation | | |

2 Are the speakers happy with the progress?

### Speaking

1 You have been asked to organize a marketing campaign to promote your company. The campaign will be by phone, by mail, and by email. You are making a list of companies to call, you have ordered some new leaflets about the company, and you have sent about twenty emails. However, the leaflets have not arrived yet, and you are still waiting for replies to your emails.

Answer your teacher's questions on the marketing campaign using phrases from Expressions where possible.

10.2

2 Now listen to a conversation role-playing the situation. Compare it to your role-play. Is the speaker happy with the progress?

### Language box

When we talk about progress, we often use the present perfect with *yet* and *already* to say which things we have done and which things we have not yet done.

> We've already planned the first phase of the project.
> We haven't contracted any new employees yet.

We use the adverbials *so far* and *up to now* to talk about our progress until the moment we are speaking.

> I've met about four customers so far.
> Up to now I haven't had time to look at your offer.

**projects**

**3** Look at the extracts from the conversation. Listen again and complete them with phrases used for updating on progress.

1 General director:   Heather, could you

_____ on the Italcafé pitch, please?

Account manager:   Well, it's

_____, actually.

2 How _____ the market research?

3 We're _____ to radio stations …

4 We've _____ for next Friday.

5 Keep me _____ .

## Writing

**1** Your colleagues have all gone on holiday, leaving you in charge of updating your small company's catalogue. Reply to the email from your boss, using the notes below.

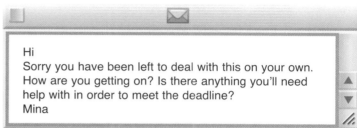

Hi
Sorry you have been left to deal with this on your own. How are you getting on? Is there anything you'll need help with in order to meet the deadline?
Mina

> **BROCHURE**
>
> PHOTOGRAPH NEW PRODUCTS – 80% done
> – ahead of schedule
> PREPARE IMAGES FOR PRINTING – 40% done
> – need help!
> WRITE PRODUCT DESCRIPTIONS – 90% done
> – fine
> CHECK TEXT – 10% done – need help!
> LAY OUT PAGES – 70% done – should be OK
> ORDER PAPER – done but not here!

We often use the expression *to meet a date / target* with the present perfect to talk about our progress.

> Unfortunately, our suppliers haven't met the date again.

> We're celebrating as our sales people have met their targets this year.

## Look

Look again at the conversations in listening scripts 10.1 and 10.2 on page 115. Find more examples of the present perfect with *yet*, *already*, *so far* and *up to now*. How many examples of *meet a date / target* are there?

# How to report success

## In this lesson you will practise different ways of announcing positive results.

### Starter

1 Today you feel very optimistic about developments at work. Tell your teacher about three things that have happened at work in the last twelve months that you are happy about.

"Well, and now the bad news!"

annie B.

### Expressions

11.1 **1** Listen to part of a meeting.

1 What is the meeting about?

2 What time of the year is the meeting taking place?

3 Is Mike pleased with the results for his department? Why?

**2** Now listen again and complete the chart with the missing information for Home Sales.

| HOME SALES (TARGET INCREASE = 12.5%) | | | | | |
|---|---|---|---|---|---|
| | JAN/MAR | APR/JUN | JUL/SEP | OCT/DEC* | TOTAL* |
| compared to last year | | | +9.2% | | +8%* |
| units sold | (6,550) | (6,830) | (6,250) | | (26,680)* |

\* = forecasted results/sales

| EXPORT SALES (TARGET INCREASE = 7.5%) | | | | | |
|---|---|---|---|---|---|
| | JAN/MAR | APR/JUN | JUL/SEP | OCT/DEC* | TOTAL* |
| compared to last year | +8.8% | | | +13.5%* | |
| units sold | (7,250) | (8,750) | (9,250) | | (32,750)* |

\* = forecasted results/sales

### Speaking

1 Report on developments in ABC Ltd for this year. Use the following chart and try to use the same language that Tony and Susan used in Expressions.

| ABC LIMITED TARGETS FOR PRESENT YEAR | | | |
|---|---|---|---|
| CONCEPT | LAST YEAR | THIS YEAR | TARGET |
| sales | $23m | $25.5m | $24m |
| profit margin | 8.4% | 9.7% | 9.5% |
| productivity | 81% | 89% | 90% |
| units sold | 31,500 | 37,350 | 35,500 |
| employee satisfaction | 78% | 89% | 85% |
| client satisfaction | 83% | 95% | 95% |
| number of new clients | 165 | 236 | 235 |
| average delivery time | 24 days | 21 days | 22 days |

projects

11.2

**3** Now listen to the export sales manager's report. Complete the chart on page 24 with the missing information for Export Sales.

**4** Now listen again. Complete the sentences below with the words she uses.

1 Well, _____ that the Export Market is doing really well.

2 I'm delighted to tell you that we have been able to sell _____ 9,000 units for the first time _____ the department, a _____ which represents an increase of 11.4%.

3 The forecast for the final quarter is also _____ .

4 Obviously, _____ about the way the department has been working this year.

5 We have _____ in eastern Europe and the new Madrid office has increased its sales by just over 20% since January, which is _____ .

## Writing

**1** You are the manager of ABC Limited. Write a short report about the results and include figures from the chart in Speaking.

## Look

Look again at listening scripts 11.1 and 11.2 on page 115. Find examples of the present perfect and past simple. Are they 'open' or 'closed' time periods?

## Language box

**Use the present perfect when speaking about 'open or unfinished' time periods:**

The results have been disappointing so far. (time period = so far)

Sales have increased by just under 10% since May. (time period = since May)

Our sales team has been working especially hard this year. (time period = this year)

**Use the past simple when speaking about 'closed or finished' time periods:**

January's figures were excellent. (time period = January)

In the same quarter last year we sold 15% more. (time period = the same quarter last year)

Between March and July, sales were slow. (time period = between March and July)

## Lesson record

| 3 new words from this lesson | 3 useful phrases from this lesson |
|---|---|
| 1 | 1 |
| 2 | 2 |
| 3 | 3 |

Things to remember

_____

_____

_____

_____

_____

_____

# How to make excuses

**12**

## In this lesson you will learn polite ways of explaining problems, delays, and mistakes.

### Starter

1 Look at the cartoon. Why does the man have the sign on his desk?

2 When did you last make an excuse?

3 When did you last hear an excuse?

### Expressions

12.1 **1** Listen to three situations where someone is making an excuse.

1 In each dialogue 1–3, what is the problem?

2 What is the excuse given?

| | problem | excuse |
|---|---|---|
| dialogue 1 | | |
| dialogue 2 | | |
| dialogue 3 | | |

**2** Listen again if necessary and rank the problems 1 (least serious) to 3 (most serious).

**3** Was it possible to prevent each problem?

### Speaking

1 Role-play the following problems, using language for giving excuses. Your teacher will play the role of the person complaining.

1 You sent a cheque to a supplier but didn't sign it. The supplier is very frustrated.

2 A letter has gone out from your department with prices in dollars instead of euros.

12.2 **2** Now listen to two conversations role-playing the situations above. Compare them to your response.

**4** Look at the extracts from the three conversations below. Complete them with the useful phrases for making excuses.

1 I _____ call, but, you know, I was having lunch with a client. We had a drink. We had to wait ages for service, and, _____ .

2 You're _____ believe it. It's _____ before, but my bus broke down on the way in.

3 I checked the content but Sue _____ do the cover, and you know, she was sick. I don't know what _____ .

## Writing

**1** Look at the business mistakes below. What excuses could you find for the errors?

> The 1982 Association of British Travel Agents conference in Phoenix, Arizona, had to change its venue at the last moment when it discovered that its original hotel had been double-booked.

source: http://jn10.co.uk/stories/funny-but-true-stories.php

> A US man was so frustrated with his laptop, that he shot it in a fit of e-rage, then realized there were important files left on it that he still needed.

source: http://news.bbc.co.uk/1/hi/technology/3193366.stm

**2** Choose one and imagine what might have caused the problem. Write the story using the past continuous.

## Look

Look again at listening script 12.2 on page 116. Find more examples of the past continuous.

## Language box

When we make an excuse, we often have to give a story explaining exactly how something happened.

We often use the past continuous at the beginning of stories to 'set the scene':

> It was snowing on that cold February morning in Chicago.

In stories, use the past continuous with the past simple when a shorter action happens in the middle of a longer one.

> Just as I was writing the cheques, we had a power cut.

You can also use the past continuous for actions happening at the same time:

> She was processing the orders at the same time as she was talking to a customer on the phone.

## Lesson record

| 3 new words from this lesson | 3 useful phrases from this lesson |
|---|---|
| 1 .................. | 1 .................. |
| 2 .................. | 2 .................. |
| 3 .................. | 3 .................. |

Things to remember

..................................................
..................................................
..................................................
..................................................
..................................................
..................................................

# How to justify change

**13**

## In this lesson you will learn to explain why changes are necessary.

### Starter

1   How often do you change your car, mobile phone, computer, or house? Normally, what reasons do you have for changing?

"Perhaps it could be a little bigger?"

### Expressions

**1**   Listen and answer the questions below.

1   Who is speaking?

2   What are they talking about?

3   What do you think will happen next?

**2**   Now listen again and complete these sentences from the conversation.

1   Do you think _____ it?

2   We simply _____ it.

3   We _____ Miami and buy a new car.

4   If we _____ a new one, we _____ go to Miami.

5   We've got no _____ get a new car.

13.2  **3**   Ali has just been visiting one of his most important clients – JPC Ltd. He returns to his office and speaks to his boss. Listen and answer the questions below.

1   Why is Ali worried?

2   Who is more worried, Ali or his boss?

3   What does Tom think they should do?

### Speaking

1   You are applying for a new job. Your friend can't understand why you want to leave your current job. Role-play the conversation with your teacher.

2   You are sales manager of a US company. You want to have a stand at an important trade fair. Your boss thinks that trade fairs are 'usually costly and not very productive'. Role-play the conversation between you and your boss. Use the language from the unit to persuade him. Here are some reasons you could use:

- make new contacts
- meet new clients
- see new developments
- show your products and services to many people at the same time
- increase your sales or clients.

### Language box

When justifying change, we often use the first conditional. The first conditional is used to talk about realistic possibilities.

The *if / unless* part of the sentence uses the present simple:

If we ask them to come to dinner, …

The other part of the sentence discusses the probable result. This uses *will*:

… we will need to arrange a taxi to take them home.

Together the two halves of the sentence make the first conditional:

If we ask them to come to dinner, we will need to arrange a taxi to take them home.

## Hint

A useful word to use when discussing options is **otherwise**, which means '**if not**':
We need to pay immediately. Otherwise we will get a fine.
You should give Yvonne a pay rise. Otherwise she will leave the company.

**4** What's going to happen in the near future?

**5** What do you think will happen in the long run?

**4** Listen again and complete the spaces with the necessary words.

**Ali:** No, Tom. I think they've made a decision about this. I think we'll simply

1 _____ set up a small plant in China near their factory. We

2 _____ to lose them as clients. And JPC is not the only client who's going to China!

**Tom:** But opening in China will cost us a small fortune!

**Ali:** Yes I know. But we simply

3 _____ do it.

4 _____ we're in trouble. I told him we'd study the question seriously. But I don't think we have

5 _____ but to open up there, and pretty quickly!

## Writing

**1** Write a short email to your boss covering the main points you discussed in Speaking exercise **2**. Explain your reasons for going to the trade fair. Write about 75 words. Write your answer in the email below.

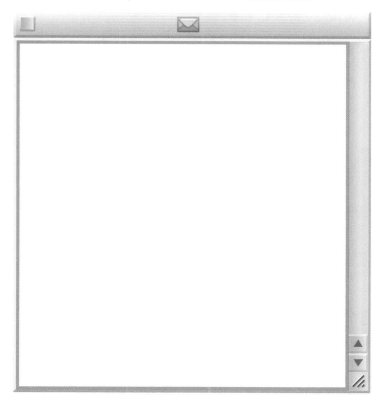

Instead of using *if*, you can use *unless* to mean *if not*.

We won't be able to finish this project if we don't get more staff.

We won't be able to afford a new IT system unless we get a government grant.

## Look

Look again at listening scripts 13.1 and 13.2 on page 116 and find further examples of the first conditional.

---

### Lesson record

| 3 new words from this lesson | 3 useful phrases from this lesson |
|---|---|
| 1 ............... | 1 ............................ |
| 2 ............... | 2 ............................ |
| 3 ............... | 3 ............................ |

Things to remember

..................................................................

..................................................................

..................................................................

..................................................................

..................................................................

..................................................................

# How to deal with people off-site

## In this lesson you will learn different phrases for liaising with clients and suppliers.

### Starter

1 What experience have you had of working with people outside your company: suppliers, freelancers, etc. (or of working in these roles yourself)?

2 Do you prefer to liaise face to face, on the phone or by email? What are the advantages and disadvantages of each?

### Expressions

14.1

1 Mansoor sells frozen foods wholesale to supermarkets. Most of his business is online. He uses a company called Webshaker to run the website and keep it up to date. You'll hear him on the phone and meeting Adam from Webshaker in person. Listen to the three short conversations.

 1 What two points does Mansoor mention in the first conversation?

 a _____

 b _____

 2 What suggestions does Adam offer in the second and third conversations?

 Suggestion in second conversation

 _____

 Suggestion in third conversation

 _____

2 Now listen again. This time complete the spaces with the words used in the recording.

 1 I tried to return your call this morning but I couldn't _____ you.

 2 So this _____ the website?

### Speaking

1 Imagine you have to deal with the following situations. Plan what you will say, and then role-play the situations as phone calls or face-to-face meetings. Your teacher will play the other role.

 1 You are waiting for some proofs of some new advertisements from the designers. They are already three days late, and you need to send them to the printers by the end of this week.

 2 You offer training courses for your staff, run by an outside training company. You would like advice on what course(s) they would recommend for improving customer-client relations. You have only got a small budget, and training should ideally take place within the next three months.

### Language box

When we are considering how things happened or didn't happen in the past, we often use a modal verb with *have* + the third form of the verb:

 I should have told you that before.

 The delivery must have been delayed.

 It would have been better to send it by post.

 I could have written the address down wrong.

**These can be used in the positive and negative:**

 I shouldn't have done it like that.

 You needn't have brought the copies.

 He wouldn't have read your email yesterday because he had the day off.

## Hint

The word **thing** is very common in informal English. Notice how it is used:

**How are things?**
**a couple of things**
**The thing is, ...**
**The main thing is ...**

3  Well, my main concern is

_____ your people

to make changes to the material we sent

you.

4  I was wondering, _____

sometime next week to talk it through?

5  The thing is, _____ at

the moment.

6  **Adam:** Listen, give me a couple of days.

**Mansoor:** OK. When

_____ ?

7  By the end of the week? What would be

the _____ you?

8  I prefer email because I'll be

_____ a lot this week ...

## Writing

1  Imagine you are Adam from the recording in Expressions. Write an email to your colleagues to update them on the outcome of the phone calls and meetings you had with Mansoor from Frozen Foods Fast.

Note that the opposite of *must have* is *can't have*:

I must have dialled the wrong number.
(= I am sure I dialled the wrong number)

I can't have dialled the wrong number.
(= I am sure I did not dial the wrong number)

## Look

Look again at listening script 14.1 on pages 116–117 and underline all the similar ways used to reflect on the past.

## Lesson record

3 new words
from this lesson

3 useful phrases
from this lesson

1 ......................

1 ......................................

2 ......................

2 ......................................

3 ......................

3 ......................................

Things to remember

.......................................................................................

.......................................................................................

.......................................................................................

.......................................................................................

.......................................................................................

.......................................................................................

# How to announce a new product

## In this lesson you will learn ways to give news about a new product.

### Starter

1  Tell your teacher about two or three new developments that have happened recently in your company.

2  In what ways are these improvements?

### Expressions

15.1 ○ 1  Listen to the first part of the meeting at AP Electronics and answer the following questions:

1  What is the man speaking about?

2  Why is the man so happy?

2  Listen again and try to write the exact words the man says.

Good morning everybody, I have

_____ for you all!

It gives me _____ that

the prototype of the new A471 ...

15.2 ○ 3  Listen to the second part of the meeting with Helen, the technical manager. She mentions several changes made from the A47 to the A471 model. Write the changes in the table below:

| A47 MODEL | A471 MODEL |
| --- | --- |
| 235 grams | |
| 16 x 4 x 3 cm | |
| 1 gigabyte | |

### Speaking

1  You work for AP Electronics and your teacher is one of your clients. Role-play the telephone conversation between the two of you. Tell your teacher about the new A471 from Expressions.

### Language box

There are many differences between the new A471 model and the old model. The following words were used to quantify these differences:

| LARGE | SMALL | PRECISE |
| --- | --- | --- |
| far | a little | five times |
| much | a bit | 25% |
| a lot | slightly | $15 |
| considerably | | |

All of these words can be used with a comparative to show a difference between two things.

It's far larger than the old model.

He's much more intelligent than the rest of the team.

The road is a lot wider than before.

After the changes, we will have a considerably smaller workforce.

**4** Peter Williams works for the Sales Department at AP Electronics. He phones a client with news of the A471. Listen to what he says.

1 What does he offer the client?

2 What is he going to do?

**5** Listen to the conversation again and write down the words Peter uses.

1 I'm phoning because I think

_____ .

2 You'll be _____ that it's much lighter and smaller.

3 Yes, but that's _____ , Chris! I'm sure you'll _____ that we can offer you a much better price!

## Writing

**1** Write two short emails about the following. Try to write about 40–50 words each time.

1 Write a short email to a client about a recent development in your company that improves its service or product. Mention the advantages of the new development.

2 Imagine Peter Williams couldn't speak to his client on the phone. Listen to listening script 15.3 again and write a short email telling the client about the new A471. Also suggest a day and time for a meeting.

The shape is a little squarer.

When you paint the room, can you make the yellow a bit brighter?

The gold model is slightly more expensive than the silver.

It's ten times quicker than last year's model.

It'll be 30% cheaper with your discount.

A double room is €30 more expensive.

## Look

Look at listening scripts 15.1, 15.2 and 15.3 on page 117, and underline all the examples of these words with comparatives that you find.

## Lesson record

| 3 new words from this lesson | 3 useful phrases from this lesson |
| --- | --- |
| 1 .................... | 1 ................................ |
| 2 .................... | 2 ................................ |
| 3 .................... | 3 ................................ |

Things to remember

........................................................

........................................................

........................................................

........................................................

........................................................

........................................................

# How to feed back on a project

**16**

## In this lesson you will learn useful phrases for giving and getting feedback on projects.

### Starter

1 Imagine you run the CD stall at the festival in the photograph. What things would you do to get as many people as possible to visit your stall and buy CDs?

2 Have you ever run a stall or stand to promote or sell something? How did it go?

### Expressions

 **16.1**

1 World Eye Records sells world music CDs and DVDs. They have just had a stand and tent to sell CDs at an open-air world music festival in Krakow, Poland. Listen to World Eye Records staff discussing how successful the festival was, and complete the table below.

| discussion point | how successful? | suggestions for next time |
|---|---|---|
| 1 NUMBER OF VISITORS | | |
| 2 SIGNING SESSIONS | | |
| 3 LEAFLET DISTRIBUTION | | |

**16.2**

2 Now listen to the same people having a meeting a week later to evaluate their participation and complete the table below.

| discussion point | how successful? | suggestions for next time |
|---|---|---|
| 1 ASIAN / MIDDLE EASTERN CDs | | |
| 2 CD SALES (LESS FAMILIAR MUSIC) | | |
| 3 LOOP VIDEO CLIPS | | |

### Speaking

1 You work for a sports equipment company. You have come back from a conference, where you were in charge of the company stand. Give your evaluation to your boss (your teacher), based on these notes, and make your own suggestions.

| notes | suggestions for next year |
|---|---|
| **LOCATION OF STAND**<br>POOR - OUT OF VIEW, NOT NEAR ENTRANCE | |
| **DISPLAY**<br>DIDN'T LOOK VERY PROFESSIONAL | |
| **PROMOTIONAL MATERIALS**<br>DIDN'T ARRIVE IN TIME | |
| **PROMOTIONAL ACTIVITIES**<br>PRODUCT COMPETITION VERY SUCCESSFUL | |
| **STAFFING OF STAND**<br>NEEDED AT LEAST ONE MORE PERSON | |

### Language box

To describe past actions, and express regret for not doing something in the past, we can use the third conditional.

The first part of the third conditional uses *if*. This explains a past possibility.

> If I'd known how many people were coming, ... (but I didn't)

> If we had invited some of our key clients, ... (but we didn't)

The second part of the third conditional uses a modal verb + *have* + past participle to explain what did not happen in the past.

> ... , I would have bought more food. (= I didn't buy more food)

> ... , the party would have been great for business. (= the party wasn't great for business)

**projects**

## Hint

**think something through** = think of all possibilities
We need to think our strategy through carefully.

**give thought to something** = consider
We must give more thought to pricing.

**rethink something** = think again
We'd better rethink our whole strategy.

**3** Listen to recording 16.1 again and complete the spaces below.

1 Jake, _____ specific numbers before next week?

2 One _____ is the papering.

3 Yes, we should _____ better in terms of quantity and distribution.

**4** Now listen to recording 16.2 again and complete the sentences below.

1 First, perhaps we _____ sales data.

2 And then _____ the website hits.

3 But I think _____ that our stock on the stand matches the festival's line up of artists much better.

4 OK. I'll make _____ for next time.

5 Well, I've got _____ by age, as well as by nationality, of all those who visited the stand.

## Writing

**1** You've just returned from a trip abroad, where you represented your company at a conference. Write an email to your boss at head office, explaining which aspects of your participation were successful in promoting your company. Include suggestions for future conference participation. Write your answer in the email below.

**2** Think of an event that you attended, for example, a training course, a conference, a festival, etc. Write feedback on the event and suggestions for improving it for the message board on the organizer's website.

The third conditional is a very difficult grammar structure to get right. When the two halves of the structure come together, the structure is very long:

If I'd known how many people were coming, I would have bought more food.

If we had invited some of our key clients, the party would have been great for business.

It might not have happened if you'd told me yesterday.

Attendance could have been better if we'd contacted our mailing list.

## Look

Look again at listening scripts 16.1 and 16.2 on page 117, and find other examples of the third conditional.

## Lesson record

| 3 new words from this lesson | 3 useful phrases from this lesson |
|---|---|
| 1 .................... | 1 .................................... |
| 2 .................... | 2 .................................... |
| 3 .................... | 3 .................................... |

Things to remember

......................................................................

......................................................................

......................................................................

......................................................................

......................................................................

......................................................................

# How to **present an idea**

## 17

## In this lesson you will learn phrases for discussing and presenting ideas.

### Starter

1  Your company has just employed twice as many staff as before. Unfortunately, there just is not enough room for everyone. Imagine you have to present a plan to the existing staff, telling them how you are going to fit all the new workers in. How can you do this in a positive way?

annie B.

### Expressions

17.1 ○ **1**  Listen to a conversation with Robin, the sales manager for Trigbee, a company selling kitchen fittings throughout the UK. In the first listening, you will hear Robin dealing with two problems put to him by his sales team, and discussing possible solutions. Complete the table below.

| | problem | solution |
|---|---|---|
| 1 | | |
| 2 | | |

17.2 ○ **2**  Now listen to Robin talking to his management colleagues about the problems his team are having and present ideas for solving them. What concerns are raised by management about his solutions?

### Speaking

1  Discuss one of the problems below. With your teacher, ask for and discuss solutions.

1  The current system for ordering stationery is not working: orders are not recorded regularly, anybody can place an order, all departments are over budget, and there is a lot of waste.

2  Your company currently has offices in New York City. The Board has decided to move their headquarters to your country and wants you to present a report on this idea.

2  Now, hold a second meeting. Present your ideas from **1** above to your management team.

### Language box

One way of adding information about a sentence is to use a relative clause:

I wanted to ask the manager, **which was impossible because he was on a sales trip.**

Sales are 60% up on last year, **which is fantastic.**

A relative clause can be used to give a reason for something:

They had never seen anything like it, **which is why they had trouble introducing it into the market.**

Sales reps have a very heavy workload, **which is the main reason people are leaving.**

meetings

## Hint

If you are discussing a list of items or problems, you can use **as for** to show that you are moving on to the next item:

**As for meetings, well, perhaps we could meet here just once a month.**

**As for** is used both in spoken and written English.

**3** Now listen to both conversations again. This time complete the spaces with the words the manager uses.

1 Well, a simple option is _____ cut the number of meetings?

2 I'd rather go straight home at the end of the day, _____ coming here to write up sales reports.

3 There have been complaints about the number of hours that they're on the road for. So _____ ideas I'd like to suggest.

4 Well, one _____ be for them to work partly from home.

5 I _____ they do some of their work from home, which I know has proved successful in other companies.

6 Oh yes. Completely. _____ to offer them is greater flexibility.

7 No, no. I mean, if I _____? The office where we work now can be used by your people in Finance.

## Writing

**1** You have just had a meeting with the management team where you put forward your ideas for solving the issues in Speaking. Write an email to those who attended, summarizing your ideas in the box below.

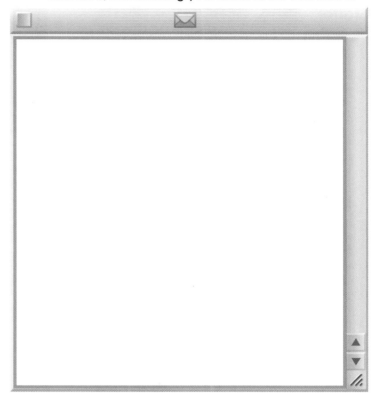

Note that in this type of relative clause, *which* is always used, and there is always a comma:

We now work on Saturdays, **which most people aren't happy about.**

Not ~~We now work on Saturdays, that most people aren't happy about.~~

Not ~~We now work on Saturdays which most people aren't happy about.~~

## Look

Look again at listening scripts 17.1 and 17.2 on pages 117–118 and underline all the examples of this type of relative clause.

## Lesson record

| 3 new words from this lesson | 3 useful phrases from this lesson |
|---|---|
| 1 .................... | 1 ................................. |
| 2 .................... | 2 ................................. |
| 3 .................... | 3 ................................. |

Things to remember

...........................................................
...........................................................
...........................................................
...........................................................
...........................................................
...........................................................

# How to **agree and disagree**

**In this lesson you will learn to show if you are in favour of, or against, an idea.**

## Starter

1  How do people show that they agree with an idea in your company or organization?

2  How much consultation should take place over important decisions?

## Expressions

18.1 ○ 1  Cormack Aluminium make aluminium products for the construction and motor vehicle industries. Listen to company owner Malcolm Cormack and heads of department Magda and Steve in their monthly meeting. Answer the questions below.

1  Magda's idea is about:

marketing / diversifying / cutting costs / food packaging.

2  What do Steve and Malcolm think of the new idea?

3  What is Magda asked to do after the meeting?

## Speaking

18.1 ○ 1  Listen to listening script 18.1 again, and imagine you are taking part in the meeting. Pause the recording and interrupt with your opinion.

2  Take turns with your teacher to give your opinion about some of these subjects. Listen to each point and then agree or disagree using some of the expressions you have just seen.

- an issue being discussed in your town
- public transport
- advertising on TV
- film censorship
- English as a world language

## Language box

Words that often occur together are called collocations. There are many different types, and some of them appear in the listening script:

**adjective + noun**

a massive demand

a growing market

conclusive reasons

**noun + verb**

a company evolves / develops / stagnates

**verb / adjective + adverb**

seriously consider

study something carefully

totally different

meetings

## Hint

**To agree** and **to disagree** are verbs in English. They are followed by **with**.
**I agree with you.**
**We don't agree with that.**
**She strongly agrees / disagrees with it.**
**Agree** is never an adjective: ~~I'm agree.~~

**2** Listen again and complete these extracts from the phone conversation.

1 With _____ Magda, it's not as simple as that.

2 By _____ , but that doesn't mean you should risk everything on a completely new product line.

3 _____ , Steve, but on the other hand, maybe we shouldn't dismiss this idea so quickly.

4 Who knows, Magda _____ , but the main problem for me is we don't know the packaging sector.

5 Sorry, Magda, I _____ .

6 I mean, _____ , but I think we should have a good look at this idea before we make a decision.

**3** Are the expressions in **2** for agreeing, being neutral, or disagreeing?

## Writing

**1** Write a short letter to a newspaper responding to the article below. Agree and disagree with things the speaker says. Try to use phrases and expressions from the unit.

When you start work, it's all very well looking down at the company car park and seeing all those BMWs , Mercedes, and Jaguars: all of them company cars driven by your bosses. You might think it's great to receive a quality vehicle just for doing your job, while you, the humble graduate trainee, have to travel to work on a crowded bus or tube. But just think: a company car isn't a free gift. In fact, in most countries, a company car is something you earn. It actually counts as part of your salary.

'So what?' you might reply. Well, just think: if you drive a very expensive car, it might push your earnings into the next tax band. You might get the car, but end up paying more tax for the privilege of driving it. Not only that, but the other problem with a company car is that it's never really yours. You can't relax in it like you would in your own machine, because one day you'll have to give it back. And if you have to leave your company, for example, if you get a job with the competition, you may have to give it back immediately, and travel back on the bus or tube with all those graduate trainees ...

**verb + noun**

    come up with reasons
    look for opportunities

**collocations with common verbs**

    make a profit
    do some thinking
    have a good look at something

Collecting collocations is an effective way of building your vocabulary.

## Look

Look at listening script 18.1 on page 118 and find more examples of collocations.

## Lesson record

| 3 new words from this lesson | 3 useful phrases from this lesson |
|---|---|
| **1** ................. | **1** ................................. |
| **2** ................. | **2** ................................. |
| **3** ................. | **3** ................................. |

Things to remember

................................................................

................................................................

................................................................

................................................................

................................................................

................................................................

................................................................

# How to **use vague language**

## In this lesson you will learn how to avoid using direct language.

### Starter

1 Have you ever had to sell anything? Did you enjoy the experience?

2 How do you feel when you speak to sales reps, either at work, at home, or on the phone?

### Expressions

1 Kenville Richards, is a manufacturer of domestic appliances. Look at the fragment from the Kenville Richards catalogue and answer questions 1–3.

   1 Why are they producing three different models of breadmaker?

   2 What is the difference between the trade price of a product and the rrp?

   3 Which product represents the best value for money?

| model | trade price | rrp | features |
| --- | --- | --- | --- |
| KR 250 | €60 | €90 | 12-hour digital timer, plastic body, maximum loaf size 16 x 16 cm |
| KR 300 | €90 | €125 | Plastic body, free bread-making book, can bake bread in under an hour, maximum loaf size 21 x 15 cm |
| KR 350 | €110 | €140 | Strong stainless steel body, designed by famous designer, complete set of breadmaking tools, maximum loaf size 30 x 15 cm |

 *19.1* **2** Carl is a sales rep for Kenville Richards. Lina is the buyer for a large domestic appliance shop. Carl has visited her to try to sell her some of the domestic breadmakers from the catalogue above. Listen to their dialogue and complete the boxes.

### Speaking

1 It is the last part of a job interview and the two sides are near to an agreement, but there are still some problems about salary, training, working on Saturdays, and a possible relocation for two years to another continent. Role-play the situation with your teacher. One of you plays the part of the interviewer and the other is the interviewee.

 *19.2* **2** Now listen to a recording of the situation from **1**. Compare it with your version.

### Language box

There are many verb phrases you can use to talk about future possibilities without giving a definite opinion. The following verb phrases may be used with *whether* or *if*:

> I'm not sure if / whether we can sell that many.
>
> I don't know if / whether we can sell that many.
>
> It's not clear if / whether we can sell that many.

You can use *depend on* in the same way, but *depend on* is followed by *whether* (not *if*).

> I don't know if I can come to the drinks before the dinner. It depends on whether my train arrives on time.

**meetings**

## Hint

In British English **quite** can mean **a bit**.
**I'm quite happy with this.** (= a bit)

In American English **quite** means **very**.
**I'm quite happy with this.** (= very)

This can be confusing for native speakers too!

| model | final price | quantity |
|-------|-------------|----------|
| KR 250 | | |
| KR 300 | | |
| KR 350 | | |

**3** Complete the extracts from the dialogue below. Then listen again to check your answers.

   **1** I _____ like them, but _____ how many we would sell here.

   **2** A lot _____ on the price.

   **3** Happy customers _____ buy another breadmaker.

   **4** It would be _____ risk for us to have a lot of expensive stock. We _____ have stock that we can't sell.

   **5** I can't say _____ . If you took about 150 ...

## Writing

**1** This is the end of your first month with a company and you think your manager has made a mistake with your pay. Write them a short email to solve the problem.

**2** A new client has just put in an order that is more than your capacity to supply at present. You want to keep the client but you need to explain by email that you need more time to deal with this order. If you can't think of a product, use the Kenville Richards breadmakers from Expressions.

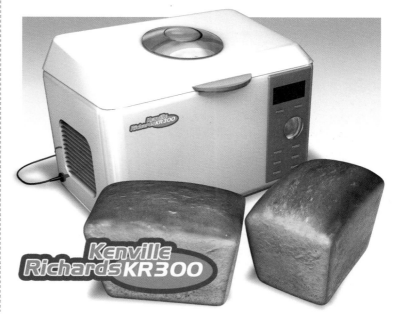

To give two (or more) future possibilities you can use *depend on whether + or*.

   It depends on whether the price is €85, €90, or €100.

   It depends on whether you want to leave early or not.

## Look

Look again at listening scripts 19.1 and 19.2 on pages 118–119. Underline more examples of vague language.

---

### Lesson record

3 new words from this lesson

**1** ....................
**2** ....................
**3** ....................

3 useful phrases from this lesson

**1** ....................................
**2** ....................................
**3** ....................................

Things to remember

....................................................
....................................................
....................................................
....................................................
....................................................
....................................................

# How to **run a meeting**

## In this lesson you will learn expressions for running a business meeting.

## Starter

1 Look at the pictures below.
   Why didn't the meetings work?

2 Tell your teacher about a meeting you have attended that didn't work. What went wrong?

## Expressions

20.1 ○ **1** Listen to the start of two meetings. For each extract answer the questions below.

   1 Is the meeting effective?
   2 Why / Why not?

20.2 ○ **2** Listen to the start and some more extracts from the second meeting. Complete the sentences below with useful expressions for running meetings.

   1 Right then, I think _____ .

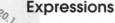

## Speaking

1 Read the agenda below.

### Managers' Meeting

To reduce costs in the IT department.

**DATE:** 3rd March 2006 **PLACE:** Meeting room 5th floor
**PARTICIPANTS:** Beatrice Martin (IT manager), Natalie Wilmot (human resources manager), Anthony Southall (CFO)

**AGENDA**
1 IT department running costs (Beatrice Martin)
2 Proposals for reducing costs (Anthony Southall)
3 Staff cuts (Natalie Wilmot)

2 Role-play the opening speech to the meeting. Use the phrases you learnt in Expressions.

## Language box

Many verbs are commonly followed by another verb. Your dictionary will tell you what form the second verb must have. Some verbs must be followed by an infinitive with *to*:

   I'm **hoping to finish** by three o'clock.
   I would **advise** you **to employ** cleaners through an agency.

Some verbs just need the infinitive without *to*:

   **Let** Paul **finish** what he's saying.

Sometimes the *-ing* form of the verb is needed:

   We can **delay making** a decision until we get the report.
   Using an agency will **save** us **interviewing** staff ourselves.

meetings

Hint

The verb **discuss** means to exchange opinions. When there is a real disagreement we use the verb **argue**. We can also use **have a discussion** or **have an argument** about something.

Hint

We refer to **an item** on an agenda.
We can talk about **item 3** or **the third item**.
We **discuss an issue** at a meeting.
We can talk about **the dress code issue** or **the sick leave issue**.

2 Now as you all know, we're

_____ the main issues

arising from the last departmental meetings.

3 As you can see, there are six

_____ .

4 Brad, could you _____

about the problems we've had with

unauthorized access to our intranet?

5 I think we need to discuss

_____ .

6 Actually, I think we should

_____ the next point

now.

7 OK, let's _____ what

we've agreed.

**3** Do you often have to attend meetings in your company? Tell your teacher about them.

## Writing

**1** A record of the discussions and decisions in a meeting is called *the minutes*. Write the minutes from the meeting in Speaking to pass to your boss for authorization. Use Anthony Southall's notes from the meeting below to help you.

> IT DEPARTMENT RUNNING COSTS: main expense rent of whole 5th floor in central office.
> Next highest - staff salaries.
>
> PROPOSALS FOR REDUCING COSTS: move IT to premises on outskirts and cut rent by 30%. Restructure to cut staff by 10%.
>
> STAFF CUTS: computer staff many years with company. Redundancy pay expensive. Any solutions? None given in meeting.

In some cases, a preposition is used before the second verb:

We have succeeded in reducing absenteeism by 30%.

Some verbs can be followed by the infinitive or *-ing* form, usually with a change in meaning:

I remember mentioning this to David last month. (= I know I did this in the past)

I must remember to mention this to David tomorrow. (= I need to do this in the future)

## Look

Look again at listening script 20.2 on page 119. Find more examples of verbs that are followed by a second verb.

## Lesson record

| 3 new words from this lesson | 3 useful phrases from this lesson |
|---|---|
| 1 .................... | 1 .................................. |
| 2 .................... | 2 .................................. |
| 3 .................... | 3 .................................. |

Things to remember

.................................................................

.................................................................

.................................................................

.................................................................

.................................................................

.................................................................

# How to **defend an idea**

# 21

**In this lesson you will learn different ways of supporting an idea.**

## Starter

1 Look at pictures a–d. They all show team-building activities. Which of these would work best in your company?

2 Have you or has anyone you know ever taken part in a similar activity? Tell your teacher about it.

3 Do you think employees learn anything from these events?

a

c

b

d

## Speaking

1 The social committee of your company is planning the 25th anniversary celebration of its foundation. They have proposed a day trip in a hot-air balloon for all staff, followed by a dinner party where the balloon is due to land. Think of possible advantages and disadvantages of this idea and tell your teacher.

2 You are a member of the social committee and your teacher is an employee who does not like the celebration you have proposed. Role-play your conversation using the useful expressions for defending an idea above.

21.2 o 3 Now listen to a similar conversation and compare it to your conversation. Did you think of the same advantages and disadvantages?

## Expressions

**21.1** **1** Listen to an extract from a meeting where someone is defending an idea.

1 What idea does Luke propose?

2 What does he say in favour of the idea?

3 What are the arguments against the idea?

**2** Complete the extracts from the meeting with useful phrases for defending an idea.

1 Why not? _____ that we have a communication problem.

2 The reason for this lack of communication is _____ that the heads of department just don't know each other well enough.

3 I'm _____ the question of time, Harry.

4 _____ we all have similar problems with organization.

5 But _____ this would be an investment for the company.

6 _____ , if we all worked together more effectively, then we would be saving the company both time and money.

## Writing

**1** Read the following email you have received from your boss.

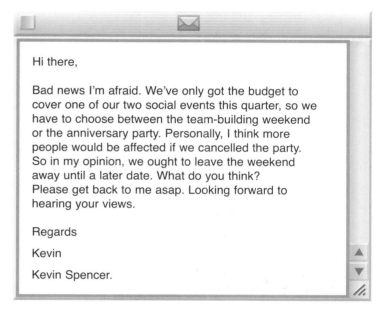

Hi there,

Bad news I'm afraid. We've only got the budget to cover one of our two social events this quarter, so we have to choose between the team-building weekend or the anniversary party. Personally, I think more people would be affected if we cancelled the party. So in my opinion, we ought to leave the weekend away until a later date. What do you think? Please get back to me asap. Looking forward to hearing your views.

Regards

Kevin

Kevin Spencer.

**2** Write an email in reply to your boss defending the idea of the team-building weekend.

## Look

Look again at conversation 21.2 on page 119. Underline the adverbs that are used.

## Language box

We often use adverbs when expressing an opinion. Sometimes, we start with an adverb to tell the listener what kind of point we are making:

**Basically**, we need to diversify.

**Quite honestly**, we have no choice.

We can also use adverbs before the verb to emphasize our opinion:

I **really** don't think we need to act immediately ...

I **honestly** believe this is our only option ...

This type of emphatic adverb would come after an auxiliary or modal verb:

I can **truthfully** say ...

I'm **quite** certain that this plan will work ...

## Lesson record

3 new words from this lesson

1 ...........................

2 ...........................

3 ...........................

3 useful phrases from this lesson

1 ...........................

2 ...........................

3 ...........................

Things to remember

..................................................................

..................................................................

..................................................................

..................................................................

..................................................................

..................................................................

# How to **speak to a group**

**22**

## In this lesson you will learn some useful expressions for speaking to groups of people.

### Starter

1   Do you have to speak to groups of people in your job? Is it difficult? Do you enjoy it?

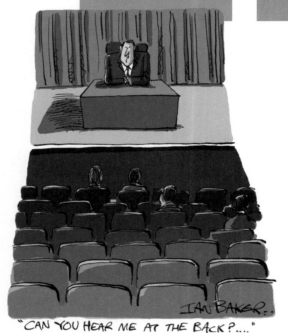

"CAN YOU HEAR ME AT THE BACK?...."

### Expressions

**22.1**

**1**  Tony works for PJK Ltd, a furniture manufacturer. Listen and answer the following questions.

1   What is Tony's job?

2   What is he doing?

3   How well does he do this?

**2**  Listen again. Look at the different things that Tony says. Write a number in the box in the order he says them.

| We can't waste time! | |
| Oh, you weren't listening, then? | |
| Be quiet please! | |
| Thanks for coming. | |
| Got that? | |

**3**  How could you say the same things in a more polite way?

**22.2**

**4**  Alvaro Garcia Ogara works in the public relations department at Marques de Laguardia, a leading Spanish wine company. Listen to Alvaro speaking to a group of visitors. Does he use similar expressions to the ones you suggested in **2**?

### Speaking

1   Your teacher is one of a group of people who are visiting the place where you work. You have to meet and welcome them. What would you say? What is important when speaking to a group?

2   Number the following points in their order of importance (1= most important). See if your teacher agrees with you.

- voice
- language ability
- preparation
- sense of humour
- knowing the audience
- eye contact
- physical appearance
- self-confidence

### Language box

We often use *which* or *that* to give details to help somebody identify something:

a company which / that makes wine

the region which / that produces the most wine

In the sentences above, *which* and *that* refer to the subject of the clause. They can also be used to refer to the object of a clause – in this case, you can leave them out if you want:

I'll give you the wine (which / that) I like best.

I hope you like the next room (which / that) we're going to show you.

*Who* is used to give details that identify a person:

people who buy this wine

the person (who) we spoke to earlier

meetings

## Hint

Some expressions to say goodbye to a group:
**I hope you have enjoyed your visit.**
**I wish you a safe and pleasant journey home.**
**It's been a pleasure to meet / meeting you.**
**I hope to see you (all) again soon.**
**Thank you (ever so much) for coming.**

**5** Here are some of the words that Alvaro uses. Listen again and see if you can reconstruct the complete expressions.

1 First of all, _____ .

2 _____ introduce myself. _____ Alvaro Garcia.

3 _____ too happy _____ .

4 _____ leave now,

5 _____ enjoyed _____ …

6 _____ wish you _____ .

## Writing

**1** You have been asked by the PR department to write a short script for a visit to the place where you work. This script will be used by all tour guides showing visitors round. Include information about who you are, what the company does, what the programme of the visit is, etc.

Write the text of the script, trying to mention as many of the following points as possible:

• welcome
• the route of the tour
• important people
• dangers (things to avoid)
• interesting facts.

*Where* can be used to give details that identify a place. *Where* cannot be left out.

the factory where they bottle the wine

Not ~~the factory they bottle the wine~~

Note that we often use *which* + preposition instead of *where*.

the factory **(which)** we bottle the wine **at**

## Look

Look at listening script 22.2 on page 120 where Alvaro explains about his company. Find five more examples of this construction. Be careful – most of the sentences leave out *which / that*.

## Lesson record

3 new words
from this lesson

1 ....................
2 ....................
3 ....................

3 useful phrases
from this lesson

1 ..............................................
2 ..............................................
3 ..............................................

Things to remember

..............................................................
..............................................................
..............................................................
..............................................................
..............................................................
..............................................................
..............................................................

# How to **structure a talk**

**23**

## In this lesson you will learn expressions for linking ideas in a talk.

### Starter

1 Look at the statements below. How true are they in your experience?

> "There's so much I want to say – I just don't know how to fit it all in."

> "An audience will forget more than 75% of what they hear within twenty-four hours."

> "I know what I want to say, but I find it difficult to present the ideas clearly and logically."

### Expressions

1 Read the following information about a central European company, and with your teacher discuss what language training options there could be.

> You have been informed that English is to become the language for all spoken and written communication within your company. Apart from one or two managers, few of your staff speak good English. However, not all staff need to use English in their job. Head office has told you that you have twelve months to make sure that all staff speak English to the level required in their job.

23.1 ○ 2 Now listen to a recording with the director of this company. What are the three training options the director mentions?

23.2 ○ 3 In the second extract, one of the options is described by an expert in detail. Listen and number the four parts of the procedure below in the correct order 1–4.

_____ analyse each post's language needs

_____ interview all members of staff

### Speaking

1 Present the introduction of one of the following talks to your teacher.

  1 You are representing your company at an international conference. What three or four pieces of information would you include about yourself and / or your company in the introduction to a presentation?

  2 Give a talk on a project you are currently working on.

  3 Give a talk on the business highlights of last year.

2 Now summarize the main points you made, and present the end of the talk to your teacher.

### Language box

When giving talks and writing formal English, we use linking words to connect ideas and help the listener or reader anticipate what is coming next. This helps communicate the message clearly to the audience. Look at the following examples:

> **In addition,** I'll summarize the company's spending on language training ...

> **First,** we interview all members of staff, as well as talking to each manager about the team under them.

Other expressions:

Giving reasons:

> *so, as a result*

Highlighting information:

> *in particular, specifically*

meetings

## Hint

It's a good idea to tell your audience at the beginning how long you'll be speaking for.
**I'll be speaking for about fifteen minutes. My talk will last about an hour.**

## Hint

It's also a good idea to tell your audience when you'd like them to ask questions.
**Please don't hesitate to interrupt if you have any questions. I'd be grateful if you could keep any questions you have until the end.**

_____ make recommendations about the training needs of each employee

_____ carry out the language testing

**4** Now listen to both extracts again. This time complete the spaces with the words used.

**Director**

1  I'd like to _____
   about language training options.

2  So, _____ a number
   of alternatives.

3  Right, so, I'll _____
   one by one.

**Language audit consultant**

4  So, I'd like to _____ to
   talk about the final stage of the procedure.

5  Right. OK then. Let me just
   _____ of the main
   points I've made.

6  Well, that's _____ at
   the moment.

"I'd like to thank you all for your attention."

## Writing

**1** You have been asked to present your ideas for improving the place where you work or study. Plan the main points you would talk about (about three or four), and the smaller points within these (about two or three in each). Write the main section of the talk in full. Try to use language from the unit to connect the points you make.

**Contrasting information:**
   *in spite of, however*

**Referring back:**
   *as I said before*

## Look

Look again at listening scripts 23.1 and 23.2 on page 120. Find more connecting expressions of this type.

---

## Lesson record

| 3 new words from this lesson | 3 useful phrases from this lesson |
| --- | --- |
| **1** ................... | **1** ................................. |
| **2** ................... | **2** ................................. |
| **3** ................... | **3** ................................. |

Things to remember

..........................................................................
..........................................................................
..........................................................................
..........................................................................
..........................................................................
..........................................................................
..........................................................................

# How to **interrupt**

## 24

### In this lesson you will learn ways to make your opinion heard.

#### Starter

1 Look at the cartoon. Is the situation familiar to you?

2 When someone is talking and you want to say something, how do you interrupt politely?

annie B.

#### Expressions

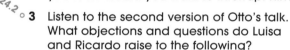

24.1 ○ 1 Serinya Textiles in Spain is now owned by Fabunder, a Swiss company. Otto, Fabunder's production manager, is visiting Serinya to communicate some news to the department heads there. Listen to Otto and mark the following sentences true (T) or false (F).

1 There's a problem with Serinya's quality control. _____

2 A Chinese company is trying to buy Serinya. _____

3 Production in Spain is going to stop. _____

4 About six Serinya people will keep their jobs. _____

2 If you were in Otto's meeting, how would you feel? Would you want to interrupt him?

24.2 ○ 3 Listen to the second version of Otto's talk. What objections and questions do Luisa and Ricardo raise to the following?

1 machinery
2 rationalizing
3 quality
4 notice period
5 orders

#### Speaking

1 Talk about your feelings and experience of the town, city, etc. you are in. Your teacher will keep interrupting politely to check or challenge what you say and to give personal opinions. Use language from the unit to deal with the interruptions and begin talking again. Then change roles.

#### Language box

When someone interrupts, we can comment positively on what they say:

That's a good point.
I see what you mean.
I take your point.

**Or we can be less positive:**

I'm really not so sure about that.
Well, there are different points of view.

**Or we can ask the person to be patient:**

I'm coming to that now / in a moment / shortly.
Please bear with me for a moment.

meetings

## Hint

When we give formal warnings about the future, this is called **giving notice**.
We are giving notice that we will be moving to Shanghai in twelve weeks.
Don't you think that twelve weeks is rather short notice?

## Hint

We also use **giving notice** to mean warning your employer that you are going to leave your job. In this case you **hand your notice in**.
Ludmilla has handed her notice in: she's going to work for the competition!

**4** Listen again. What solutions and answers does Otto give to the objections from Luisa and Ricardo in **3**?

**5** Listen again and complete the spaces with the expressions used to interrupt.

  **1** **Luisa**: Excuse me, _____ interrupt?

  **2** **Ricardo**: Otto, sorry, _____ rationalize, ...

  **3** **Ricardo**: _____ , Otto. Did you say we're going to be closed down?

  **4** **Luisa**: Excuse me, Otto, _____ ? Are you so sure about the quality?

  **5** **Otto**: _____ finish? Obviously, we'll keep ...

## Writing

**1** Listen to Otto's final words in the second version. You are Luisa or Ricardo. Reply to Otto's final suggestion in a formal email outlining your position (you agree to work with him / you are so upset you will resign / you give a noncommittal answer).

**2** Write a short text about the situation in recording 24.1 from the point of view of the Chinese manager of the new factory near Shanghai.

**Or we can just finish what we want to say:**

As I was saying, ...
May I just finish?
If I can just finish.

## Look

Look again at listening script 24.2 on page 121 and find more examples of dealing with interruptions.

---

**Lesson record**

| 3 new words from this lesson | 3 useful phrases from this lesson |
|---|---|
| **1** ................ | **1** ................................ |
| **2** ................ | **2** ................................ |
| **3** ................ | **3** ................................ |

Things to remember

...........................................................................
...........................................................................
...........................................................................
...........................................................................
...........................................................................
...........................................................................

# How to **meet for the first time**

**In this lesson you will learn useful expressions for meeting people.**

## Starter

1 Which of the following happens to you the first time you meet someone?

I talk too much because I'm nervous.

I don't speak at all because I can't think of anything to say.

I smile a lot so that the other person likes me.

I act in exactly the same way as I would with a person I know.

2 Can you remember when and where you met some of the following people for the first time? Tell your teacher what happened.

- a very good friend
- your boss
- a girlfriend / boyfriend
- a colleague
- a customer
- a teacher

## Expressions

1 Listen to the conversation between two people meeting at a conference, and complete the table below.

|  | speaker 1 | speaker 2 |
|---|---|---|
| name |  |  |
| country |  |  |
| department |  |  |
| now? |  |  |

2 Look at the extracts from the conversation. Complete them with the useful phrases for meeting people for the first time.

1 Nice _____. I'm Sofia Platini from Milan.

2 Pleased _____, Sofia.

3 Is this your _____ to London?

4 It's the second time _____, actually.

## Speaking

1 Invent the missing information in the table below and role-play a similar conversation with your teacher.

|  | speaker 1 | speaker 2 |
|---|---|---|
| name | Sam Isaakson | Chris Richter |
| country | Sweden | Germany |
| job | Accountant | PA to the director |
| now? |  |  |

2 Now listen to a similar role-play with the people above and compare the conversations. Were your ideas the same for each job?

## Hint

When we start a sentence with **It's the first /
second time** ..., we use the present perfect.
It's the first time I've come to this conference.

## Hint

Use the following for responsibilities at work:
**I'm in charge of ordering stationery.**
**He runs the IT department.**
**She's the head of Human Resources.**
**They're responsible for overseas marketing.**

5  What _____
   Fernando?

6  _____ your flight,
   Sofia?

7  Fine, no problems. _____ ?

## Writing

1  Read the following email and reply to it, attaching a
   brief article about yourself for the company
   newsletter.

Dear all,

In an effort to bring all staff together within the
company, we are inviting you to submit a brief
article about yourself and your function within the
group. Over the next week or so, a member of our
editorial team will be visiting each and every one of
you to take photos and collect your comments.
Thank you for your help

Best wishes

Ana Fernández
Editor, In-house newsletter.

## Look

Find more examples of the present continuous in
listening scripts 25.1 and 25.2 on page 121.

## Language box

We use the present continuous for actions we
are doing now or at the moment.

   We're working on a presentation.
   She isn't enjoying the conference.
   Are they talking about the new legislation?

We also use the present continuous for more
temporary actions:

   I'm staying in a hotel near the conference
   centre.

Some verbs are not commonly used in the
continuous form.

   It looks like we're going to start.

We use the present simple for more permanent
actions:

   I work in the centre of Tokyo, but I don't live
   there.

## Lesson record

| 3 new words from this lesson | 3 useful phrases from this lesson |
|---|---|
| 1 ................ | 1 ................................................. |
| 2 ................ | 2 ................................................. |
| 3 ................ | 3 ................................................. |

Things to remember

................................................................
................................................................
................................................................
................................................................
................................................................
................................................................

# How to **catch up**

**26**

In this lesson you will learn expressions to find out what people have been doing since you last met.

## Starter

1   Representatives of many Pacific countries are meeting in Japan for their biennial conference. This is the welcoming cocktail event. What do you talk about when you meet colleagues who you haven't seen for a year?

2   Do you wait for people to ask you questions or do you take the initiative yourself?

3   How comfortable are you at large social events that you have to attend for work?

## Expressions

26.1 ○  **1**   Listen to the conversation between Masako, Heather, and Sue. What do they talk about? Write *yes* or *no* in the column for conversation 1.

|  | conversation 1 | conversation 2 |
|---|---|---|
| their journey to Kyoto |  |  |
| their children / families |  |  |
| their work |  |  |
| their academic studies |  |  |
| their houses and homes |  |  |
| their hobbies |  |  |

26.2 ○  **2**   Now listen to another conversation at the conference, between Ku-duk, Carlton, and Miguel. What do they talk about? Write *yes* or *no* in the column for conversation 2.

**3**   Look at the extracts from the second conversation below. Complete them with useful phrases for catching up.

1   Good to see you again, Ku-duk, Miguel. How _____ ?

2   Now I know what I have to say when I give my talk tomorrow. But _____ me.

## Speaking

1   Imagine you meet an international colleague who you haven't seen for a year. Try to mention all the topics in the table in Expressions. Ask them what they've been doing and answer their questions.

2   After not seeing them for six months, what three things would you say to a close friend, and what three things to an acquaintance?

## Language box

To talk about an activity that started in the past and may be continuing in the present, we can use the present perfect continuous:

We've been looking for a house to buy.
And I've been travelling quite a bit.

To talk about an activity that started in the past and is still continuing, we can use the present perfect continuous with *for*, *since*, or *How long*?:

I haven't been sleeping very much since he was born.

I've been doing a course in traditional calligraphy for six months, and it's going well.

And how long have you been learning Russian for?

**socializing**

**Hint**

If you **talk shop**, it means you talk about work in a social situation.

**After the meeting, we went out to dinner to get to know each other, but all they did was talk shop.**

3 I hardly had time to sit down. So _____ last year?

4 I've been taking a lot of photos of him. Ku-duk, what _____ to?

5 And what's _____ , Carlton?

## Writing

1 An old school or university friend asks you in an email what you have been doing. Answer their email and ask them some questions too.

2 Your manager has asked you to send him an email outlining how you have been spending your time at work during the last month.

To talk about a completed activity or event that happened in this recent space of time we are talking about, we can use the present perfect simple:

I've finally finished my doctorate.
I've become a father.

## Look

Look again at the conversations in listening scripts 26.1 and 26.2 on pages 121–122. Find more examples of the present perfect simple and continuous.

**Lesson record**

| 3 new words from this lesson | 3 useful phrases from this lesson |
| --- | --- |
| 1 ............... | 1 ............................... |
| 2 ............... | 2 ............................... |
| 3 ............... | 3 ............................... |

Things to remember

................................................................
................................................................
................................................................
................................................................
................................................................
................................................................

# How to **tell a story**

**27**

## In this lesson you will practise expressions used for telling stories.

### Starter

1 Which is the best airline you have ever flown with? Which is the worst?

2 With your teacher, brainstorm all the different things that could go wrong when you fly.

### Expressions

1 Listen to David telling a story about something that happened to him while travelling. Which two pictures best describe what happened?

### Speaking

1 Tell your teacher about something strange that happened to you, (or to a friend of yours) while travelling.

2 Ask your teacher to tell you a story. Be prepared to interrupt and ask questions to find out more details, especially about the background situation.

### Language box

To put a story into a time and situation context, we usually begin with the past continuous:

> We were travelling from Oslo to Kiev.
> I was living in Bilbao at the time.

We can also use the past perfect:

> I had just finished my university degree.
> She had been to Brazil before, but I hadn't.

We can use the past continuous to describe the immediate background to an event:

> Everyone was getting nervous, but then the police arrived.
> We were taking off when the plane began to shake.

**socializing**

## Hint

**2** Look at the extracts below. Complete them with useful expressions for telling a story.

1   Joanne:   Have you ever had a frightening experience on a plane?

   David: _____ .
A couple of years ago.

2   _____ outside the plane it was suddenly like a disaster movie – _____ , flashing lights, sirens, people running around.

3   To _____ , I continued reading my book. I mean, there was nothing I could do.

4   Later – the food, _____ , was out of this world – _____ , later, ...

5   But _____ we had no further problems, so we _____ got to Tokyo over twelve hours late.

## Writing

**1** Imagine you are David from Expressions. When he was at the hotel, he had time to send an email to his friend explaining the delay. Write the email.

**2** You are the co-pilot of the plane. You have to send an emailed report to head office in Athens to explain your delay. Write the email.

**3** Write about a dangerous situation you found yourself in.

## Look

Find more examples of the past continuous and the past perfect in listening script 27.1 on page 122.

But the main part of the story, if it follows a chronological order, is in the past simple:

   So I got on the plane, sat down, and put my seatbelt on.
   I asked them if I could use their phone.

When we want to interrupt a story to mention something that happened before, not afterwards, we use the past perfect:

   I suddenly realized that I had left my passport at the hotel.
   The customs officer asked me if I had packed my bag myself.

## Lesson record

| 3 new words from this lesson | 3 useful phrases from this lesson |
|---|---|
| 1 .................... | 1 ........................................ |
| 2 .................... | 2 ........................................ |
| 3 .................... | 3 ........................................ |

Things to remember

...........................................................................

...........................................................................

...........................................................................

...........................................................................

...........................................................................

...........................................................................

...........................................................................

# How to **describe someone else**

## In this lesson you will learn how to describe the personality of other people.

### Starter

1   How does your company recruit people?

2   Read this article about Chris Jones. Do you agree with his opinion?

### EUROPEAN INDUSTRY NEEDS MORE 'CHARACTER', EXPERT WARNS

'European industry needs to give as much importance to the character and personality of its managers as it gives to their qualifications!' claimed business consultant Chris Jones at the annual conference of Human Resources Managers in Birmingham yesterday. 'When selecting staff for top positions, companies should first identify the ideal personality profile that the job requires. It's not enough to be just well-qualified and hard-working – other qualities are equally, if not more, important. The modern manager must be imaginative, outgoing, communicative, and innovative in order to succeed in modern business.

### Expressions

1   Look at the following adjectives. They all describe a person's personality. Is each word positive, negative, or could it be both? Use ✓, ✗, or ✓ / ✗.

| | | | |
|---|---|---|---|
| easy-going | **single-minded** | bossy | **open-minded** |
| **narrow-minded** | enthusiastic | **sociable** | goal-oriented |
| practical | **charming** | inconsistent | **analytical** |
| **understanding** | self-confident | **supportive** | ambitious |

2   Take it in turns with your teacher to define these words. Try to guess the word. Look at the following examples:

**easy-going**: I think this is a positive word. These people are not difficult to work with. They are flexible, cooperative, and so on.

**single-minded**: This word could be positive or negative. It can be a good thing to concentrate on only one objective or thing, but this word also describes somebody who does this too much.

### Speaking

1   What qualities or characteristics are important in your line of work?

2   Your company needs to employ new staff. Discuss with your teacher what personality profile would be suitable for each of the posts below.

   • chief accountant
   • telephone salesperson
   • training manager
   • maintenance technician
   • sales rep
   • receptionist in the front office
   • laboratory technician

### Language box

We often use *make / let / allow / get* to show how one person affects the actions of another. Notice their different grammatical patterns:

*make* + somebody + infinitive (no *to*)

   She makes everyone contribute, especially at meetings.

   She makes you want to do a good job.

*let* + somebody + infinitive (no *to*)

   He lets you take your own decisions.

   They didn't let me leave the meeting early.

*allow* + somebody + infinitive with *to*

   He won't allow you to change your targets.

   She allowed me to take a short holiday.

## Hint

Be careful with these three questions:
**What is Peter like?** (= personality)
**How is Peter?** (= health)
**What does Peter look like?** (= appearance)

## Hint

You can use negative forms to be less direct:
**She's not very hard-working.** ( = she is lazy)
**He's not the fastest learner.** ( = he is slow)
**He's not exactly charming.** ( = he is rather aggressive or impolite)

28.1

**3** Listen to four people describing their new managers.

1 First write the adjectives they use to complete column A.

2 Now listen again. How do the four speakers describe the qualities of their managers? Complete the sentences in column B. The first is an example.

| A | B |
|---|---|
| 1 _____ | She's got everybody working well. She always lets you know _____. |
| 2 _____ | She lets _____ if she thinks they're good. She doesn't allow anybody _____. |
| 3 _____ | He wouldn't allow _____. He's got us all talking _____ and money. |
| 4 _____ | He makes everybody _____ at work. He lets you do things _____. |

## Writing

1 Choose two of the jobs from Speaking and write two short texts describing the appropriate personality profile for each job. Use the language in the example below to help you.

### Personality profile

A chief accountant must be a patient and practical person. They are responsible for the company accounts and should be goal-oriented and capable of working under pressure. Good communication skills are required. The accountant must be analytical and capable of independent work.

*get* + somebody + *-ing*

She's got us making suggestions and coming up with ideas.

The new manager has got us working twelve hours a day!

## Look

Find more examples of *make*, *let*, *allow*, and *get* in listening script 28.1 on page 122.

## Lesson record

| 3 new words from this lesson | 3 useful phrases from this lesson |
|---|---|
| 1 _____ | 1 _____ |
| 2 _____ | 2 _____ |
| 3 _____ | 3 _____ |

Things to remember

_____
_____
_____
_____
_____
_____

# How to **make, accept, and decline offers**

**29**

## In this lesson you will learn phrases for making and accepting offers, and polite ways of declining offers.

### Starter

1   Read the email below sent between two friends. What would you do in this situation?

**Subject:** My problem

Hi Yvonne
As the project manager for our advertising company, I have commissioned a top artist to design a series of posters for us. The problem is that our office is in London, and the designer, Thor Rosen, lives in Norway. I need to meet Thor to discuss the project, and he has invited me to meet him at his home in Bergen. But Thor is a great entertainer, and if I meet him in his home, we'll spend a lot of time in pubs and restaurants and meeting friends. We should meet in London, where we'll get a lot more work done. But I don't want to upset him at the start of the project. What do you think?
Mark

### Expressions

29.1  1   Listen to six short conversations. For each one, decide what the offer is, and whether it is accepted (✓) or declined (✗).

| | offer | ✓ / ✗ |
|---|---|---|
| 1 | | |
| 2 | | |
| 3 | | |
| 4 | | |
| 5 | | |
| 6 | | |

2   Now listen again. This time complete the spaces with the words used.

1   Jamie:   We're going to the Irish pub.

Susan:   Sounds like a nice idea.

_____ , thanks.

### Speaking

1   Look at the following situations. Decide if you would be more likely to accept or decline them (and if so, why). Then role-play them with your teacher.

1   A client has taken you to meet colleagues of his at a reception. At the end, he offers you a lift back home. You think he has had too much to drink.

2   You are at an international conference. After the opening reception dinner, one of your clients suggests going to a nightclub. Tomorrow you are giving the opening plenary at the conference.

29.2  2   Now listen to two recordings of the situations above. Compare them with your answers.

### Language box

Two phrases that are often used for referring to an unreal situation are *if only* ... and *I wish* ... Look at the following examples.

If only he was more enthusiastic.
(= but he isn't)

If only she answered my emails.
(= but she doesn't)

I wish you were coming with me.
(= but you're not)

I wish you could stay longer.
(= but you can't)

Notice that in these examples the speaker refers to a situation in the present, but uses the past simple tense.

socializing

**Hint**

When declining offers, it's usually polite to give a reason, excuse, or explanation. You can use the following to introduce the excuse:

**Actually, I'd prefer to ... / I'd rather ...**
**I'm afraid I've got to ...**
**Thanks, but I've already / just ...**

2  Oh, um. _____ another copy? It won't take a moment.

Er, no, actually. _____ .

I've got a copy at the office.

3  Oh, you can't make it – that's a pity!

No, _____ . I'm away at a wedding.

4  Well, would a drink help?

_____

a brandy perhaps?

Oh, I wish I could have one! But

_____ .

It's fine, thanks.

5  Oh, _____ a taxi?

I'd rather walk. But yes, _____ .
A taxi would be great.

6  Oh, that's such a shame! Oh, go on, Tim.

No, really _____ .
Thank you.

## Writing

1  For each of the following offers, write an email to accept, and another to decline.

1  You have received an email inviting you to open an exhibition in town next month. It clashes with your daughter's school parents' evening. You really do not like the artist's work, but you do not want to let them down, and feel it could be a useful business opportunity.

2  You have been asked to give a talk at a conference early next year in Frankfurt to promote your products or services. The previous week you will be in Hong Kong, and the week after you will be in Cairo. You know that one of your competitors will have a large stand at the conference.

Another expression that uses the past tense to refer to the present is *It's time*:

It's time they left. (= they should leave now)

It's time he sent us the contract. (= it's late)

Notice that you can also use the infinitive when you are talking about yourself or someone else.

It's time to go now.

## Look

Look again at listening script 29.1 on pages 122–123, and underline all similar examples.

---

**Lesson record**

3 new words from this lesson

3 useful phrases from this lesson

1 ........................  1 ........................................

2 ........................  2 ........................................

3 ........................  3 ........................................

Things to remember

........................................................................
........................................................................
........................................................................
........................................................................
........................................................................
........................................................................
........................................................................

# How to survive on the phone

## In this lesson you will learn expressions to use when taking a telephone message.

### Starter

1 What difficulties do you have when using the phone in English?

2 Have you ever had to deal with a difficult phone call?

COULD I HAVE YOUR NAMES PLEASE?

SURE. THEY'RE MERINDA MACMANAMAN AND AINHOA ASTIGARRAGA-ARRANZABAL.

IAN BAKER

### Expressions

30.1

1 Mandeep Bains works for an airline catering service in Singapore. Their business is supplying in-flight meals to airlines. She receives a phone call at her office. Listen to the two parts of her telephone conversation and correct the message below.

> Jackie Westinghouse rang on Monday.
>
> Her company has problems with their phone lines, so we cannot get information about flights NOA 567 departing Singapore to San Francisco at 09.45 on Sunday, and flight NOA 1145 leaving at 23.30 the next day.
>
> She will email passenger numbers.

2 None of the phrases below appear in the conversations. Listen to the phone conversations again, and write down the language used instead of each phrase below.

Say that again.

### Speaking

1 You answer a colleague's phone at work. Your teacher will play the part of somebody who has to ask your colleague a favour. Take the message.

2 Your teacher phones to change the date, time, and venue of your next English class. Note down the details in your diary.

### Language box

A phrasal verb is a two- or three-part verb. The second part of the verb changes the meaning of the verb. Compare:

I'm giving him the job.

I'm giving up my job.

Phrasal verbs are especially common in spoken English. Some phrasal verbs can be separated when used with a pronoun (*him, her, it, them*, etc.):

... you're not going to be able to access our database until our engineers **sort** it **out**.

If a noun is used with this type of phrasal verb, it can come inside or after the verb:

... until our engineers **sort** the problem **out**.

... until our engineers **sort out** the problem.

## Hint

It can be very difficult to hear the difference between numbers 13–19 and 30–90. To check which number you heard, ask this question:
**We need fifty computers.**
**Was that five-o or one-five?**

There is this problem.

Don't speak so fast!

I don't know your name.

The letter 'e'.

Do you understand?

I don't understand.

I understand.

Repeat that information.

## Writing

1 Follow up the message you looked at in the Expressions section. You are Mandeep, and you have to send an email to the head of logistics, Lee Pheng, reporting all of the information from the call.

## Look

Look again at listening script 30.1 on page 123. Find more examples of phrasal verbs.

**Other phrasal verbs cannot be separated, whether used with a pronoun or noun:**

... we **depend on** this for exact passenger numbers ...

... we **depend on** the database for exact passenger numbers ...

**Others do not take an object:**

**Hang on** – was the last time three-zero or one-three?

**Your dictionary will tell you whether a phrasal verb is separable, inseparable, or does not take an object.**

## Lesson record

| 3 new words from this lesson | 3 useful phrases from this lesson |
|---|---|
| 1 ................... | 1 ................... |
| 2 ................... | 2 ................... |
| 3 ................... | 3 ................... |

Things to remember

.........................................................

.........................................................

.........................................................

.........................................................

.........................................................

.........................................................

# How to phone around

## In this lesson you will practise different telephone conversations.

### Starter

1 Complete this questionnaire about telephone habits, then talk your teacher through your answers.

1 How many hours do you spend on the phone in a typical working day? _____

2 Do you make more calls, or receive more calls?
make ☐   receive ☐

3 Which do you use most, a mobile or a landline?
mobile ☐   landline ☐

4 How do you feel when answering the phone at work?
completely relaxed ☐
less comfortable than speaking face-to-face ☐
anxious ☐

5 How often do you make a phone call purely for pleasure?
often ☐   sometimes ☐   rarely ☐   never ☐

6 How do you feel if you do not have your mobile phone with you?
relaxed ☐   a little uncomfortable ☐
very uncomfortable ☐   I always have it ☐

7 How would you describe your phone use outside work?
too much ☐   about right ☐

### Expressions

1 Della is to trying to find a replacement speaker for a conference on health and safety at work. She is phoning the National Association of Builders.

*31.1* 1 Listen to the first conversation, and answer the following questions.
  a What department does Suzanne work for?
  b What advice does she give to Della?

*31.2* 2 Listen to the second conversation and answer the following questions.
  a When is the talk happening?
  b What does the man recommend?

*31.3* 3 Listen to the third conversation and answer the following questions.
  a What help does Peter James give?
  b What number does he give to Della?

*31.4* 4 Listen to the fourth conversation and answer the following questions.
  a What money does Della offer to pay?
  b What do Della and Alastair agree to do?

2 Look at the extracts from the four telephone calls below. Complete them with the phrases used by the speakers.

1 I don't know if you _____
  but I'm organizing a conference about

### Speaking

*31.3* 1 Listen to the third conversation between Della and Peter James again and look at the notes below. Try to reconstruct the conversation with your teacher. Change roles when you finish.

Della  Tell Peter who you are, and why you are phoning (you want him to speak at a conference).

Peter  You would like to give the presentation but you are busy. You suggest your colleague Alastair Wilkins does it instead. Alastair is not in his office, so you give Della his mobile number: 564 77 0808.

### Language box

The present continuous is used to describe things that are happening at the time of speaking, or to refer to fixed events in the future:

He isn't working today.

We are increasing the number of branches in eastern Europe.

I'm meeting some people at 9.30 tomorrow.

About 500 people are coming to the conference next month.

Some verbs are not usually used in the present continuous tense:

I don't like my new office.
(not ~~I'm not liking~~ ...)

We need more space.
(not ~~We are needing~~ ...)

## Hint

Note that the verbs **telephone**, **phone**, **call** and **ring** do not use the preposition **to**.
I phoned ~~to~~ Tom last night.
I'll call ~~to~~ Mary and ask her.
I'm going to ring ~~to~~ head office.

## Hint

You can use the preposition **for** if you need to request a service:
**Can you call for a taxi please?**
**I don't want to cook. Let's phone for a pizza.**

You can use the adverb **back** if you return a call:
**Can he phone me back, please?**

Health and Safety at Work. I'm _____ someone who could give a talk about the new safety standards.

2   I'm interested _____ someone who could give a talk.

3   Do you know who I _____ or what department could help?

4   I'm putting _____ now.

5   My name's Della Wilson from A&G Construction. I was _____ your PR department.

6   I have just been speaking to a _____ who said I should speak to you.

7   I understand. I'd really _____ if you could recommend someone else, though.

8   I got your number from Peter James, who said that you _____ .

9   The _____ I'm phoning

is _____ I'm organizing a conference about Health and Safety at Work.

3   Now listen to all four conversations again and check your answers to **2**.

## Writing

1   Write the short email that Della sends to Alastair Wilkins. In your email thank him for agreeing to speak at the conference and include the most important details about the conference. Remind him about the phone call at 11.00 tomorrow.

Many of these verbs are connected with thinking and understanding:

> I see what you mean.
> The design looks old-fashioned, if you ask me.

Sometimes a verb can be used in the simple or continuous form, depending on the meaning:

> I think you've done a great job! (= opinion)
> What are you thinking about? (= action)

These verbs are known as stative or state verbs. The most common are: *think, know, forget, understand, remember, have (= own), own, like, dislike, love, hate, need.*

## Look

Find examples of stative verbs in listening scripts 31.1 to 31.4 on pages 123–124.

# How to **order, and check an order**

## In this lesson you will learn some expressions for placing an order with a supplier.

### Starter

1 The following adjectives describe food. Which ones describe taste? Which ones describe texture?

| fruity | dry | sweet | hard |
|---|---|---|---|
| bitter | creamy | salty | soft |
| crumbly | sharp | light | tangy |

2 Which of the words in **1** can describe cheese? What is your favourite type of cheese?

### Expressions

1 Rosie Elder is a cheese importer based in New Zealand. She is telephoning her Dutch supplier, Kristina Van Deer. Listen to their telephone conversation and answer the questions below.

　1 Why is Rosie having problems placing her order?

　2 What quantity of the following cheeses does Rosie order?

Mature Edam _____

Young Edam _____

Low-fat Gouda _____

Large Maasdam _____

2 Listen to the rest of the conversation between Rosie and Kristina, and answer the questions below.

　1 Why does Kristina ask Rosie to re-send her order by email?

　2 How many boxes of cheese in total will Rosie receive?

### Speaking

1 You are a wine merchant phoning a New Zealand wine maker to place an order. You have a budget of €3,000 to spend. Look at the information in the table below and role-play the phone conversation. Your teacher will be the New Zealand wine maker. Try to use question tags. One case contains twelve bottles.

| Wine type | Number of cases available | Price per case | Comments (stock, delivery, etc.) |
|---|---|---|---|
| Chardonnay | 100 | €52.50 | Was €60.00 |
| Sauvignon blanc | 75 | €70.00 | Only 15 cases available now, the rest next month |
| Cabernet Sauvignon | 60 | €40.00 | Will be sent next month |
| Pinot noir | 35 | €47.50 | |
| Merlot | 25 | €40.00 | |
| Riesling | 5 | €80.00 | Total price of €350 if all cases are bought |

telephoning

## Hint

We can say **to ship** even if the transport is by air, road, or rail.
**We can ship the goods anywhere in the world in seven days.**

**3** Listen again to these extracts from the two conversations. Complete the sentences with expressions for placing and checking orders.

1 Yes that's right, send me four boxes of mature Edam _____ .

2 No problem. I've got _____ .

3 I'd like to _____ order for Gouda.

4 Can you wait until next week for those? We're a bit _____ stock.

5 Right, Kristina, _____ the order now.

6 I just want _____ everything.

7 Plus North Holland extra mature: two boxes. _____ , isn't it?

## Writing

1 Look at listening scripts 32.1 and 32.2 on pages 124–125. You are Kristina. Send an email to Rosie confirming her order.

2 Look at the table of wine information in Speaking. Imagine you are emailing the wine exporter to make an order. Your budget is €4,000. Write a formal email.

## Language box

Often when we check information or express surprise, we can use question tags.

**Positive beginning, negative tag:**
We will meet them on Thursday, won't we?

**Negative beginning, positive tag:**
There isn't money available, is there?

The tag agrees with the tense of the main verb. But use the verb *to do* if there is not an auxiliary verb at the start of the sentence:
He likes dancing tango, doesn't he?

## Look

Find more question tags in listening script 32.1 and 32.2 on pages 124–125.

## Lesson record

3 new words from this lesson

1 ........................
2 ........................
3 ........................

3 useful phrases from this lesson

1 ........................
2 ........................
3 ........................

Things to remember

...........................................................
...........................................................
...........................................................
...........................................................
...........................................................
...........................................................

# How to **discuss documents on the phone**

## In this lesson you will practise how to discuss and correct a document over the phone.

### Starter

1 You arrive at work and see this notice on the notice board in reception. What's your reaction?

**MEETING AT 10
TO DISCUSS THE QAULITY
OF OUR PRODUCT'S.
ITS IN ROOM 4.**

2 How do you check that documents are correct before you print or send them?

### Expressions

1 Read the letter to a new client called Paul Howick. This letter was prepared by Jeff for his boss, David Jones. What changes would you make to the letter?

Dear Paul

I am writing to say thanks for your fantastic hospitality during our recent visit to your installations (great lunch!). We thought your new production line was great.

We want you and your assistant production manager, Sarah Davies, to visit our main manufacturing factory in Manchester next month. Please tell us the best dates for you.

Best wishes

David Jones
SALES MANAGER

 **2** Listen to David speaking to Jeff and see if the changes he suggests are similar to your suggestions. Read the corrected version to your teacher when you finish.

 **3** Phil works for a company called Camp & Trek, which sells camping equipment by mail order. He has prepared a new format for the order form in the company's catalogue. He asked Janet to proofread the new document and to suggest any changes. Listen to their conversation and mark the changes on the order form on the right. There are ten changes in total.

### Speaking

1 Your name is David Harper, marketing manager of Camp and Trek Ltd. You don't like the new design of your business card (below). Change or correct five things and then role-play a telephone call with your teacher, who has designed the new card. Tell your teacher about the changes and give reasons when necessary.

**HARPER**, DAVID
MARKETING MANAGER

TEL: 0191 498 1012
FAX: 0191 498 1021

**CAMP & TREK**

**OUR SATIS\        . OBJECTIVE**

EMAIL: dharper@campandtrek.com
ADRESS: Snowdon House, Tark Lane,
Durham DH4 5LY GREAT BRITAIN

### Writing

1 You are Paul Howick. Write a suitable reply to the letter from David Jones in Expressions exercise 1. Include the date and time for your visit to his company.

telephoning

**Hint**

Some common expressions when asking people to change things in a document are:
**Could you change X to Y / replace X with Y?**
**I think Y sounds better than X.**
**Could you put Y instead of / rather than X?**
**Delete X and put Y.**

## ORDER FORM

### CAMP & TREK

**HOW TO ORDER:**

PHONE 0191 498 1010      FAX 0191 498 1021
WEB www.campandtrek.com      EMAIL sales@campandtrek.com
POST Camp and Trek, Snowdon House, Tark Lane, Durham, DH4 5LY

NEW CUSTOMER?  YES ....  NO ....    CUSTOMER N°. ..........................

ADDRESS   Title .............   First name ...........................
          Surname...................................................
          Address .................................................
          Postcode ................... Daytime Tel: .................

Do we have your email address to keep you informed of the progress of your order as well as confirming shipping dates? We will also keep you informed of any product updates or special offers.
Email ...............................................

We can only ship goods to the registered credit card address (to which your invoice is sent). Please check that the address provided is correct and that you have included your postcode.

| PAGE N° | CATALOGUE CODE | DESCRIPTION | SIZE |
|---|---|---|---|
| 42 | QR 211343 | TREKKING POLES | - |

| COLOUR | QTY | INDIVIDUAL PRICE | TOTAL PRICE |
|---|---|---|---|
| RED | 2 | 20.25 | 40.50 |

**4** Listen again and complete the phrases below.

1 The typeface is a bit too big. _____ a little smaller.

2 Well, I think it _____ in the top left-hand corner of the page.

3 And I _____ colour for the logo.

4 But I think _____ these two lines at the bottom of the page.

5 And _____ put eight boxes for the customer number.

6 You could _____ for where they have to write their email address in the middle of the form.

7 It's difficult to read the note about the credit card address. Can you _____ a lot bigger?

8 Well, I'd _____ each of these columns into two.

## Language box

The following prepositions are commonly used to refer to a place in a document.

| | |
|---|---|
| in | the diagram / picture |
| | the second line down |
| | the third paragraph |
| | the top left-hand corner |
| | the left-hand margin |
| on | page 2 |
| | the right-hand side |
| | the other side of the page |
| at | the top / bottom of the page |
| | the beginning of paragraph four |
| | the end of the second line |

## Look

Find examples of these prepositions being used in listening script 33.1 and 33.2 on page 125.

## Lesson record

| 3 new words from this lesson | 3 useful phrases from this lesson |
|---|---|
| 1 ................ | 1 ................................ |
| 2 ................ | 2 ................................ |
| 3 ................ | 3 ................................ |

Things to remember

...........................................................
...........................................................
...........................................................
...........................................................
...........................................................
...........................................................

# How to complain on the phone

## In this lesson you will practise different expressions for complaining over the phone.

### Starter

1 Look at this list of practical advice for complaining about goods or services. Six sentences are from an official leaflet, the other four are false. Which are false?

1 Stay calm, even if you are angry.
2 Be clear about what you want while remaining polite, and never aggressive.
3 Before making a complaint, find out if you have a friend or relative who knows the owner.
4 Back up claims in writing where possible.
5 Keep records – this includes copies of all receipts, letters, and emails. Never send original documents – send copies.
6 When complaining in person, always speak in a loud voice so that other customers can hear your conversation.
7 Complaining in person can be more effective – ask to speak to the person in charge. There is no point losing your temper, especially if the person cannot authorize action.
8 If you are not offered an immediate solution, take a pen and say in a loud voice, 'and what's your name'?
9 If you complain on the phone, keep records of who you spoke to and when, and what was said. Always follow up calls with a letter.
10 If there is no immediate response to your first complaint, pass the matter on to your lawyer. Take legal action!

### Expressions

34.1

1 John Harris makes three telephone calls. Listen to each call and complete the table below.

| company called | reason for call | action |
|---|---|---|
| Ealing Taxis | | |
| Fastpost Services | | |
| ISO Camera Centre | | |

2 Tell your teacher about each call. How would you describe John Harris's mood?

### Speaking

1 With your teacher role-play the following telephone calls. Use the plan to make two different calls for each situation.

1 You ordered some materials which are a month late and still have not arrived.
2 You have received an invoice for an order which was cancelled a month ago.

company welcome, give company name
customer give name, explain call
company respond – get personal details
customer give details
company say there is nothing you can do
customer ask to speak to someone else
company say manager is not there
customer protest, ask when manager back
company give information
customer end call

### Language box

You can use *ever* and *never* with the present perfect to express your strong feelings about a situation. These situations may be negative:

I've never had to wait so long before!

This is the slowest service I've ever had!

We've never been refused credit with you before!

This is the first time we've ever been refused credit with you!

Or positive:

I've never had such a delicious lemon tart!

This is the most delicious lemon tart I have ever had!

telephoning

## Hint

Note that we complain **about** something **to** somebody.
I've complained to the IT help desk about their slow response.

We **make** a complaint, and sometimes complain **in writing** / write **a letter of complaint**.

**3** Listen again to the conversations and complete them with the useful phrases for complaining.

**Conversation 1**

1 Great – thanks for that. It's _____ , I'll be waiting outside the house.

**Conversation 2**

2 But you've _____ made a mistake. We made it _____ clear that we wanted the express service.

3 Well, you _____ modify the invoice for this delivery.

4 And could you please make sure that this sort of thing _____ ?

5 Well, it's _____ time we've had this problem.

**Conversation 3**

6 No. No. Another month is _____ question.

7 I'll be making a _____ about this.

8 I'm sorry to go on about it, but this is _____ .

**"I definitely ordered fifty boxes of carrots!"**

## Writing

1 Imagine John Harris writes a letter to Fastpost Services in the second part of recording 34.1, instead of telephoning. Write the letter explaining the reason for the complaint and that this is not the first time something like this has happened. Say that you will change to a different courier if this happens again.

---

Note that *such* needs an indefinite article with a countable noun, but not with an uncountable or plural noun:

I've never experienced such a long delay!

I've never come across such bad service before!

I've never seen such poorly trained staff!

## Look

Look again at listening script 34.1 on pages 125–126, and find examples of the present perfect with *ever* and *never*.

---

## Lesson record

| 3 new words from this lesson | 3 useful phrases from this lesson |
|---|---|
| 1 .................... | 1 .................... |
| 2 .................... | 2 .................... |
| 3 .................... | 3 .................... |

Things to remember

......................................................
......................................................
......................................................
......................................................
......................................................
......................................................

# How to write emails for the first time

## 35

## In this lesson you will learn how to write a first email to a business contact.

### Starter

1 What things do you have to think about when writing an email to someone you have not met or emailed before?

2 What kind of 'first time' emails do you receive? How does the subject line help you deal with these?

### Expressions

1 Read the emails below. For each, choose the best subject line.
1 a Office designs – London
b Meeting – your office
c Anton Berg – new offices

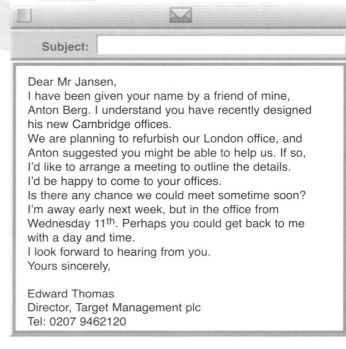

**Subject:**

Dear Mr Jansen,
I have been given your name by a friend of mine, Anton Berg. I understand you have recently designed his new Cambridge offices.
We are planning to refurbish our London office, and Anton suggested you might be able to help us. If so, I'd like to arrange a meeting to outline the details. I'd be happy to come to your offices.
Is there any chance we could meet sometime soon? I'm away early next week, but in the office from Wednesday 11th. Perhaps you could get back to me with a day and time.
I look forward to hearing from you.
Yours sincerely,

Edward Thomas
Director, Target Management plc
Tel: 0207 9462120

### Practice

1 Using the language in Expressions and in the Language box, write one of the following emails. Invent any details you need. This is the first email.

1 To Hans Mauer, car-leasing, to request a test-drive of a car for your office use. Offer to telephone at a time suitable for him.

2 To Anna Pavlova, requesting a demonstration of a new intercom system. You have her name from a friend, Sergei Blokhin, whose offices have had this installed. Offer to telephone at a time suitable for her.

2 Now follow up your email by telephoning Hans or Anna. Your teacher will be Hans or Anna. Find out about: times, costs, address of your business correspondent.

### Language box

Emails often have a simple structure. Below are some example phrases commonly used in emails.

**How to start**

Further to our phone conversation, ...
You may remember ...
Thank you for sending ...
With reference to ...,
I have been advised to contact you ...

**New information**

As you may be aware, ...
We're hoping to ...

2   a   Brussels Conference
    b   Programme changes
    c   Theatre tour, USA

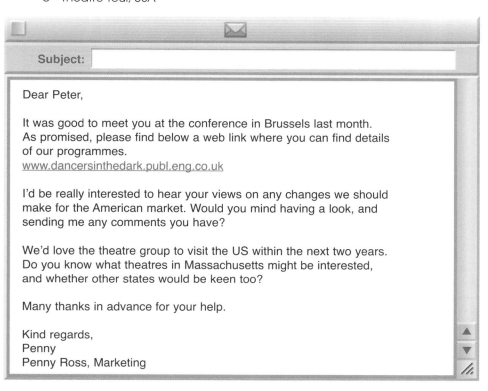

**Subject:**

Dear Peter,

It was good to meet you at the conference in Brussels last month.
As promised, please find below a web link where you can find details of our programmes.
www.dancersinthedark.publ.eng.co.uk

I'd be really interested to hear your views on any changes we should make for the American market. Would you mind having a look, and sending me any comments you have?

We'd love the theatre group to visit the US within the next two years. Do you know what theatres in Massachusetts might be interested, and whether other states would be keen too?

Many thanks in advance for your help.

Kind regards,
Penny
Penny Ross, Marketing

## Action

I'd be grateful if you could …
Would you be able to … ?
Please let me know …

## Friendly sign-off

Thank you again for your help.
I hope to hear from you soon.

## Look

Find other phrases from the emails to add to those in the Language box, and include any more you know.

# How to write a formal email

## In this lesson you will practise different expressions to use in a formal email.

### Starter

1 Would you write a formal or an informal email in the following situations?

1 Agreeing to meet a colleague for lunch.

2 Complaining to a supplier about a mistake in an order.

3 Requesting information from an official website.

4 Attaching the agenda for a meeting in an email to a colleague abroad.

5 Apologizing for a delay in delivery to a customer.

6 Sending your boss a report.

2 How would you start each email?

annie B.

## Expressions

1 Read the emails below and explain why the writers use a formal style.

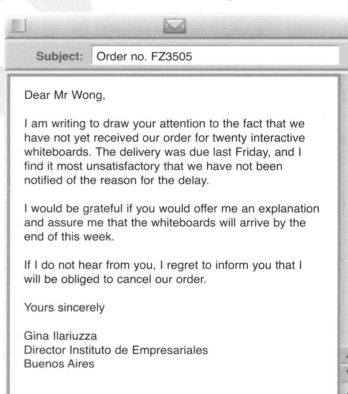

**Subject:** Order no. FZ3505

Dear Mr Wong,

I am writing to draw your attention to the fact that we have not yet received our order for twenty interactive whiteboards. The delivery was due last Friday, and I find it most unsatisfactory that we have not been notified of the reason for the delay.

I would be grateful if you would offer me an explanation and assure me that the whiteboards will arrive by the end of this week.

If I do not hear from you, I regret to inform you that I will be obliged to cancel our order.

Yours sincerely

Gina Ilariuzza
Director Instituto de Empresariales
Buenos Aires

## Practice

1 Using the language in Expressions and in the Language box, write this email in a more appropriate style. Invent any extra information you need.

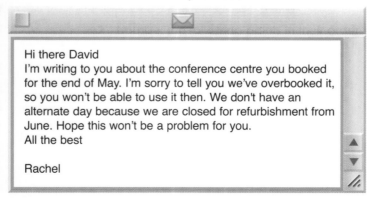

Hi there David
I'm writing to you about the conference centre you booked for the end of May. I'm sorry to tell you we've overbooked it, so you won't be able to use it then. We don't have an alternate day because we are closed for refurbishment from June. Hope this won't be a problem for you.
All the best

Rachel

2 Now telephone Rachel in response to her email. Your teacher will be Rachel.

## Language box

Formal emails have a number of features which are not present in more friendly emails. Firstly, the vocabulary is more formal:

I am afraid I will not be able to attend the meeting on Friday.

Not ~~I'm sorry I can't make the meeting on Friday.~~

### We tend to use fewer phrasal verbs:

If any problems arise ...
Not ... ~~problems come up~~ ...

We will test the prototype ...
Not ... ~~try out the prototype~~ ...

They may eventually sell ...
Not ... ~~end up selling~~ ...

The phrases are often longer and more complicated:

email

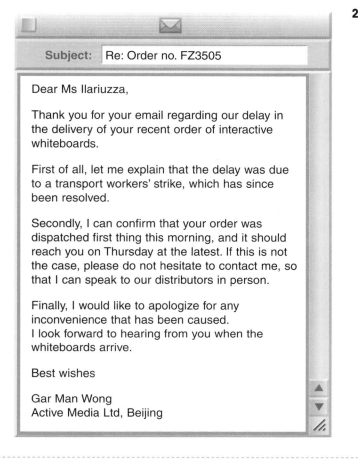

Subject: Re: Order no. FZ3505

Dear Ms Ilariuzza,

Thank you for your email regarding our delay in the delivery of your recent order of interactive whiteboards.

First of all, let me explain that the delay was due to a transport workers' strike, which has since been resolved.

Secondly, I can confirm that your order was dispatched first thing this morning, and it should reach you on Thursday at the latest. If this is not the case, please do not hesitate to contact me, so that I can speak to our distributors in person.

Finally, I would like to apologize for any inconvenience that has been caused.
I look forward to hearing from you when the whiteboards arrive.

Best wishes

Gar Man Wong
Active Media Ltd, Beijing

**2** Read the emails again and write the formal equivalent next to these informal expressions.

1   Please get in touch.

_____

2   I'm not happy.

_____

3   Thanks for your email about ...

_____

4   Please ...

_____

5   I'm sorry for any problems.

_____

6   We sent your order ...

_____

7   I'm sorry to tell you ...

_____

8   I'm writing to let you know ...

_____

We will not transfer the amount on the invoice until we have received our complete order in perfect condition, however long that may take.

### We normally do not contract the verb forms:

I am writing to inform you that I will not be in the office on Monday as I have a doctor's appointment.

Not ~~I'm writing to tell you I won't be in on Monday because I'm going to the doctor's.~~

### We often use the passive:

Your invoice will be sent next week.

I was told we would receive a 10% discount.

## Look

Look again at the two emails in Expressions and underline all the features of formal emails.

# How to be friendly in an email

## 37

## In this lesson you will practise expressions to use in an informal / friendly email.

### Starter

1  Who do you exchange friendly emails with at work? Who was the last one to / from?

2  How do you make an email sound friendly rather than just business-like?

### Expressions

1  Read the emails below quickly and add a subject line. Summarize what they are about to your teacher. Why are the emails being sent?

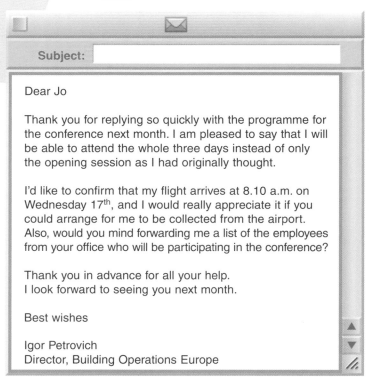

**Subject:**

Dear Jo

Thank you for replying so quickly with the programme for the conference next month. I am pleased to say that I will be able to attend the whole three days instead of only the opening session as I had originally thought.

I'd like to confirm that my flight arrives at 8.10 a.m. on Wednesday 17th, and I would really appreciate it if you could arrange for me to be collected from the airport. Also, would you mind forwarding me a list of the employees from your office who will be participating in the conference?

Thank you in advance for all your help.
I look forward to seeing you next month.

Best wishes

Igor Petrovich
Director, Building Operations Europe

### Practice

1  Write one of the following emails, using the language from Expressions and the Language box.

1  To Noriaki Kasagi, product manager of a tyre factory in Japan. You want to tell him the dates of the Automobile Exhibition in Detroit and find out if he wants you to arrange a hotel for him.

2  To Marisol, a Peruvian friend who you are hoping to meet at the IberAmerican conference you are in charge of next month. You are enclosing the conference information and you want to meet one night for dinner.

2  Now follow up your email by telephoning Noriaki or Marisol to make the necessary arrangements. Your teacher will be Noriaki or Marisol.

### Language box

You can often omit *I*, *I'm*, and *It's* in a friendly email:

Can't make the meeting on Monday.

Had a nightmare journey home last night.

Will call you tomorrow after lunch.

Not sure if you got my last email.

Pleased to hear you got back safely.

Good news about the L'Oréal pitch!

**Sometimes you can omit the verb clause completely:**

Great night last night!

More news tomorrow.

email

## Hint

To make a good impression on the person you are writing to, use a suitable greeting and sign-off:

| | |
|---|---|
| Dear Philip | All the best |
| Hello Fatima | Yours sincerely |
| Hi there Jacques | Kind regards |
| | Best wishes |

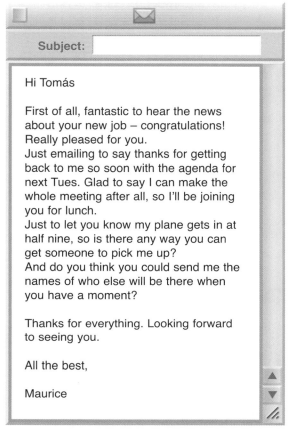

Subject:

Hi Tomás

First of all, fantastic to hear the news about your new job – congratulations! Really pleased for you.

Just emailing to say thanks for getting back to me so soon with the agenda for next Tues. Glad to say I can make the whole meeting after all, so I'll be joining you for lunch.

Just to let you know my plane gets in at half nine, so is there any way you can get someone to pick me up?

And do you think you could send me the names of who else will be there when you have a moment?

Thanks for everything. Looking forward to seeing you.

All the best,

Maurice

**2** The following table shows some phrases you can use to be friendly in both formal and informal emails. Find the corresponding phrase and complete the table.

| formal and friendly | informal and friendly |
|---|---|
| **GREETING** | |
| .............................................. | .............................................. |
| **OPENING REMARK** | |
| .............................................. | Thanks for ... |
| **GIVING INFORMATION** | |
| I'd like to confirm ... | .............................................. |
| **MAKING A REQUEST** | |
| .............................................. | Can you ...? |
| .............................................. | Could you ...? |
| **CLOSING REMARK** | |
| Thank you in advance for all your help. | .............................................. |
| I look forward to seeing you next month. | .............................................. |
| **SIGN OFF** | |
| .............................................. | .............................................. |

In most cases the word *that* can also be omitted:

Just to let you know (...) I'm thinking about your proposal.

Sorry to hear (...) you're leaving the company.

## Look

Look again at the second email in Expressions and underline all the examples of shortened sentences you can find.

---

**Lesson record**

| 3 new words from this lesson | 3 useful phrases from this lesson |
|---|---|
| **1** .................... | **1** ........................................ |
| **2** .................... | **2** ........................................ |
| **3** .................... | **3** ........................................ |

Things to remember

..................................................................

..................................................................

..................................................................

..................................................................

..................................................................

..................................................................

# How to **explain in other ways**

**38**

## In this lesson you will learn expressions to use when there has been a misunderstanding.

### Starter

1 Match the possible captions to the cartoons below. Choose the best caption for each cartoon.

That is, although this is a high-priority job, we weren't expecting you to do it alone.

What we're looking for here is an idea that will really jump out at us.

In other words Stevens, you're fired.

In fact, I'm not much of an animal lover myself.

2 What do you think the misunderstanding has been in each situation?

### Expressions

1 Read the two emails on page 79 and decide what the misunderstanding is in each case.

2 Complete the two emails with the phrases below.

| First email | Second email |
|---|---|
| In other words | In fact, |
| What we're really looking for here | we were not expecting |
| I meant | To give you an example, |
| To put it another way, | That is |
| When I said | what we had in mind |

### Practice

1 Write one of the following emails using phrases from Expressions and the Language box.

1 To Carmen Souza, graphic designer, Porto. You asked her to design a new logo for your company, but her design is unsuitable. Write an email explaining to her what you really wanted.

2 Your company's small staff took a week's holiday while Johnson's Removals moved your office furniture to new offices. You left clear instructions, but you have returned to discover that they completely misinterpreted you.

2 Now follow up your email by telephoning Carmen or Mr Johnson to set a new deadline for their work and to make sure they understand their brief.

## Hint

**I expect she'll come.** = It is very probable she will come.

**I hope she'll come.** = I want her to come but I don't know if she will.

**I'm waiting for her to come.** = I know she is coming but she is not here yet.

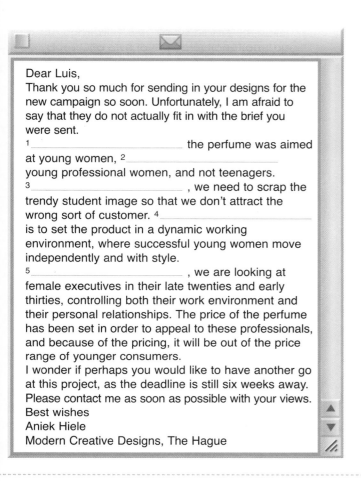

Dear Luis,

Thank you so much for sending in your designs for the new campaign so soon. Unfortunately, I am afraid to say that they do not actually fit in with the brief you were sent.

1_____ the perfume was aimed at young women, 2_____ young professional women, and not teenagers.

3_____ , we need to scrap the trendy student image so that we don't attract the wrong sort of customer. 4_____ is to set the product in a dynamic working environment, where successful young women move independently and with style.

5_____ , we are looking at female executives in their late twenties and early thirties, controlling both their work environment and their personal relationships. The price of the perfume has been set in order to appeal to these professionals, and because of the pricing, it will be out of the price range of younger consumers.

I wonder if perhaps you would like to have another go at this project, as the deadline is still six weeks away. Please contact me as soon as possible with your views.

Best wishes
Aniek Hiele
Modern Creative Designs, The Hague

Dear Francesca,

Thank you for your mail attaching your proposal for the menu for our 25th anniversary dinner. Unfortunately, your offer is not exactly

1_____ because it does not quite fit into our financial requirements.

2_____ , although we requested an impressive dinner including a wide variety of dishes, 3_____ the cost to exceed €2,400.

However, we are extremely interested in working with you on this event and we would like to propose that you make some changes to the menu so as to bring it into line with our budget.

4_____ , the white truffles in the starter could easily be replaced by wild mushrooms in garlic sauce, and this would halve the price. 5_____ , we are looking at spending about €60 per head on this meal and we are sure you will be able to fulfil this requirement for us.

Thank you in advance for your help in preparing what is, for us, an extremely important event.

Yours sincerely
Gerald Schulz
Basic Solutions Ag, (St Gallen (CH) Office)

## Language box

When you are explaining a purpose for doing something, you can use the infinitive with *to*:

> We need to take a shorter lunch break to bring us into line with Europe.

You can also use *in order to* and *so as to*:

> You'll have to finish the project by Friday in order to get it to me the following Monday.

> I was hoping for a more modern design so as not to attract the wrong type of clients.

You can also use *so that* + subject and verb:

> I'd like a wide choice of dishes so that there's something for everyone.

## Look

Look again at the two emails in Expressions, and underline the phrases of explanation.

## Lesson record

| 3 new words from this lesson | 3 useful phrases from this lesson |
|---|---|
| 1 ................... | 1 ................................... |
| 2 ................... | 2 ................................... |
| 3 ................... | 3 ................................... |

Things to remember

.................................................................
.................................................................
.................................................................
.................................................................
.................................................................
.................................................................

# How to write forceful emails

## In this lesson you will learn expressions for making your message stronger in emails.

## Starter

**assertive** /əsɜːtɪv; (US) əsɜːrtɪv/
expressing something strongly and with confidence

**assess** /əˈses/ to estimate the nature, quality or value of something

1   Which of these sentences do you think are assertive, and which are aggressive? What's the difference?

There are some concerns being raised with the standard of your work.

I won't be spoken to like that – I'm never going to shop in your stores again!

Please send me a full refund, and remove my name from your mailing list.

Take your car out of our car park and don't put it there again!

Your staff are useless – get rid of the lot of them.

As a result, we have no option but to terminate the contract.

2   What assertive emails have you had to write? Have you ever written or received an angry email?

## Expressions

1   Read the emails on page 81. For each one, choose the best subject line.

email 1   a   Complaint
          b   German conference
          c   Feedback – Düsseldorf

email 2   a   Christmas brochures
          b   Printing
          c   Late proofs

2   The following expressions help the reader understand how the parts of an email are linked. Put them in the numbered gaps in the emails on page 81:

Additionally

Firstly

so that

As you will appreciate

Consequently

However

therefore

## Practice

1   Using the language in Expressions and in the Language box, choose appropriate phrases to write one of the following emails. Invent any information and details you need.

1   Write an email to the office manager of the neighbouring business, complaining that their staff continue to park in the spaces allocated for your office.

2   Write an email to the manager of an advertising company you have been using for several years. They place adverts all over town for your firm, but these are regularly covered up with new adverts (placed by the same company) before the allocated advertising period is over.

## Language box

When writing a forceful email, you can use these phrases to get the recipient's attention:

I am writing to remind you that …

I feel you should be made aware of…

I would like to point out that …

You can use these phrases to make the consequences of the problem clear:

This has resulted in …

This has led to …

This has caused …

As a consequence / result of this …

## Hint

You can use an adverb to emphasize an adjective or a verb:
**completely** unreasonable / unexpected
**absolutely** crucial / vital / essential
**extremely** important / disappointing
We **fully** understand / intend ...

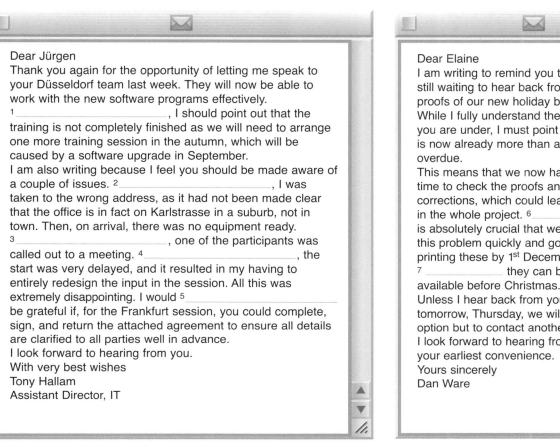

Dear Jürgen

Thank you again for the opportunity of letting me speak to your Düsseldorf team last week. They will now be able to work with the new software programs effectively. 1_____, I should point out that the training is not completely finished as we will need to arrange one more training session in the autumn, which will be caused by a software upgrade in September.

I am also writing because I feel you should be made aware of a couple of issues. 2_____, I was taken to the wrong address, as it had not been made clear that the office is in fact on Karlstrasse in a suburb, not in town. Then, on arrival, there was no equipment ready. 3_____, one of the participants was called out to a meeting. 4_____, the start was very delayed, and it resulted in my having to entirely redesign the input in the session. All this was extremely disappointing. I would 5_____ be grateful if, for the Frankfurt session, you could complete, sign, and return the attached agreement to ensure all details are clarified to all parties well in advance.

I look forward to hearing from you.

With very best wishes
Tony Hallam
Assistant Director, IT

Dear Elaine

I am writing to remind you that we are still waiting to hear back from you with proofs of our new holiday brochures. While I fully understand the pressure you are under, I must point out that this is now already more than a week overdue.

This means that we now have very little time to check the proofs and make corrections, which could lead to a delay in the whole project. 6_____ it is absolutely crucial that we can rectify this problem quickly and go ahead with printing these by 1st December 7_____ they can be made available before Christmas.

Unless I hear back from you by midday tomorrow, Thursday, we will have no option but to contact another company.

I look forward to hearing from you at your earliest convenience.

Yours sincerely
Dan Ware

---

**Make clear what the consequences will be if there is no action:**

> If immediate steps are not taken to rectify the situation, we will be forced to consider legal action.

> Unless we receive the parts by Friday, it will be necessary to contact another agent.

> Please send us assurances that this will not happen again, otherwise we will have no option but to cancel the contract.

## Look

Look again at the two emails in Expressions, and underline all the phrases of this type.

# How to **book**

**40**

## In this lesson you will learn some useful expressions for making arrangements.

### Starter

1 How often do you have to travel for professional purposes?

2 Who organizes your travel arrangements?

3 Has there ever been a major problem with your travel arrangements?

### Expressions

40.1 ○ **1** Mike and Sarah work for a printing company near Manchester, England. Listen to them discuss Mike's travel arrangements, and complete the table below.

| date of meeting? | |
|---|---|
| place? | |
| length of meeting? | |

40.2 ○ **2** Now Sarah phones Four Seasons Travel to book Mike's trip. Look at the sentences below from her conversation. Find and correct one mistake in each sentence.

1 I need return tickets and accommodations for my colleague Michael Wise.

2 Can you get me a fly to Boston on the 26th?

3 Do you know what hotel he wants to live in?

4 Manchester to Boston, departing 09.15 arriving in Boston 15.15 local hour.

5 That's with a changeover at Newark.

6 I'll put him on the wait list and see.

**3** Now listen to the conversation between Sarah and Lucy again and mark each sentence below true (T) or false (F).

1 The company Mike and Sarah work for is called DEL Graphics. _____

2 Sarah wants Mike's hotel to be in the centre of town but inexpensive. _____

### Speaking

1 Make a phone call to a travel agent to arrange flights and accommodation for a business trip to two different cities, with one night in each city.

2 Phone the travel agent from **1** again, because you now have to spend two nights in the first city.

3 Now make a final phone call, confirming these arrangements.

### Language box

Prepositions of time and place follow various patterns:

| | place |
|---|---|
| **on** | with planes, trains, ships, buses: You'll be on flight AZL 449. I'll get on the 8.45 from Victoria Station. |
| **at** | for a place that is a point on the map: Which hotel will you be staying at? I'll have to change planes at Heathrow. |
| **in** | for cities, countries, etc: I'll be staying in Los Angeles for a week. When will you be back in Ireland? |

travel

## Hint
You arrive **in / at** a place (not **to**).
**What time do you arrive in New York?**
**We arrived at the hotel at six.**

3  She books the flights. _____

4  There's a problem with the return to Britain on the 28<sup>th</sup>. _____

40.3 ○ **4**  Lucy phones Sarah back with Mike's travel details. Listen to their phone conversation and complete these extracts.

1  He _____ on BLE flight 466 to Boston via Newark on the 26<sup>th</sup>.

2  In Boston _____ at the Liberty Inn on the 26<sup>th</sup> and 27<sup>th</sup>.

3  I _____ all the prices to you this afternoon.

4  You _____ on Monday 26<sup>th</sup> on BLE flight 466, departing from Manchester at 09.15.

5  You _____ at the Liberty Inn for the two nights.

**5**  What do you notice about the future forms in **4**?

## Writing

**1**  Email your travel agent, telling them your schedule for a business trip. Ask them to book your flights and hotels.

**2**  Your teacher wants to reschedule a class next week. By email, explain your schedule and suggest possible times when you could do the class.

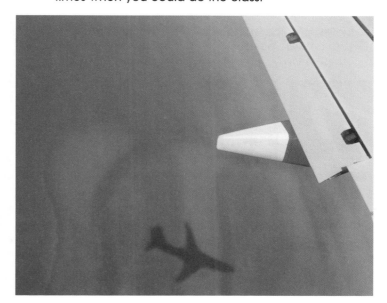

## Look

Look at listening script 40.1 and 40.2 on page 126 and underline the examples of time and place prepositions.

| time |
|------|
| **for dates or days:**<br>We won't be working on 1<sup>st</sup> May.<br>I'll see you on Wednesday! |
| **for an exact time, or with night:**<br>I arrive at 10.15 p.m.<br>They won't see anything at night. |
| **for a part of the day:**<br>She's leaving early in the morning.<br>In the evening we'll go out for a drink. |
| **To say how long before something happens:**<br>I'll call you back in a while. |

# How to **check in and check out**

## In this lesson you will practise the phrases you need to check into and out of a hotel.

### Starter

1  Look at the following pictures of hotel facilities. Which would you expect to find in your hotel if your company sent you on a business trip?

2  Which of these hotel facilities are the most important for you? Tell your teacher.

### Expressions

1  Look at the conversations of a guest in a hotel. Find five mistakes in each.

Good night. I have a reservation.
**Good evening. What name is it, please?**
Carbalho, Paolo Carbalho.
**How long are you staying, Mr Carbalho?**
I'm staying during two nights.
**OK. You're in room 312 on the third floor. Here's your key card.**
Aaah. How this works?
**Well, once you've opened the door, you have to insert it into the slot in the wall to turn on the electricity in your room.**
Right. And does it also activate the air-conditioning?
**Yes. The air-conditioning comes on as soon as you put the card in the slot.**
Fine. You think could you give me a wake-up call tomorrow morning?
**Yes, certainly. What time?**
At 7 o'clock, please.
**Of course.**
And what time is breakfast?
**Breakfast is served from 7 to 10, and lunch from 12 until 2.**
Right.
**Do you need any help with your luggage?**
No, it's all right thanks. I can manage. Could you tell me where is the lift?
**Yes, it's just at the end of the passageway. Enjoy your stay at the Imperial Hotel, Mr Carbalho.**

### Speaking

1  Role-play checking into a hotel. You have a reservation for a double room for three nights at the Hotel Suisse in Lucerne. You need to know if there is a safe in your room and how it works. You would like to have dinner in the hotel and you need an alarm call every morning at six o'clock. Your teacher will be the receptionist.

2  Role-play checking out of the same hotel. You've had a couple of things from the minibar, and, unfortunately, you dropped a bottle of champagne. You have also made several calls home. You would like to pay by credit card, and you need a taxi to go to the railway station. Your teacher will be the receptionist.

### Writing

1  Write a short review of your stay in the Imperial Hotel, Ljubljana to post on their website. Include your opinion about your room, the food, the service, and the location of the hotel. Invent any details you need.

**Hint**

When we give a piece of information that we are not sure about, we can use the verb **appear**:
**It appears that the meeting isn't going to happen.**
**It appears to be missing.**

"
Good morning. I like check out, please.

**Good morning, Mr Carbalho. Did you enjoy your stay?**

Yes, the room was very comfortable. I'm afraid I have problem with the remote control for the television, though. It fell in the bath last night while I was getting out, and it doesn't appear to be working now. I'm terribly sorry.

**Don't worry, Mr Carbalho. We'll sort it out. Thank you for telling us. Did you have anything from the minibar?**

Yes, I had one bottle of mineral water and any beer.

**How many bottles?**

Just one. And I also made two telephone calls to Lisbon.

**Right. I'll just add that to your bill. That's €354.25, please.**

I pay by American Express?

**Yes, of course.**

Here's my card.

**Thank you. Could you sign here, please?**

Of course. Would it be OK my bags here? My plane doesn't leave until later this afternoon, and I want to do a bit of shopping before I leave Ljubljana.

**Yes, certainly. Just bring them into the office, and you can leave them as long as you like.**

Thank you. I'll be back at about 3 o'clock to pick them up.
"

41.1

**2** Listen to the conversations and check you found the ten mistakes.

**3** Complete the useful expressions for checking into and out of a hotel.

1 Good _____ . I _____ reservation.

2 I'm staying for _____ .

3 How _____ this _____ ?

4 Do _____ call tomorrow morning?

5 Could you tell me where _____ ?

6 Good morning. _____ please.

7 I'm afraid _____ with the remote control.

8 I had a bottle of mineral water and _____ .

9 Can _____ American Express?

10 Would it be OK _____ here?

## Language box

We use *a / an* when we mention something for the first time:

I'd like a double room with a bathroom.

Is there a lift?

When it is clear what we are referring to, use *the*:

The restaurant is at the end of the road.

Use *one* to specify quantity:

We drank one bottle of wine, not two.

We use *the* with hotels, but not with the name of an airport or station:

Take me to the Hilton Hotel at Rome Airport.

## Look

Look again at the conversations in Expressions and find examples of articles.

**Lesson record**

3 new words from this lesson

3 useful phrases from this lesson

1 ........................    1 ........................

2 ........................    2 ........................

3 ........................    3 ........................

Things to remember

..................................................
..................................................
..................................................
..................................................
..................................................
..................................................

# How to **check a route**

## In this lesson you will learn how to check directions.

### Starter

1 Some people say that men never want to ask for directions when they are lost. What is your opinion? What do you do?

2 Are you good at giving directions? What are good directions?

### Expressions

42.1 ○ **1** Two Chinese Americans, Jun and Wei, are visiting Sydney, Australia. They are at Central Station. Listen to their conversation and mark the places and streets mentioned on the map on page 87.

42.2 ○ **2** Now listen to two conversations where Jun and Wei are checking their route. Write the expressions they use.

**Conversation 1**

1 Excuse me, is this _____ The Harbourside?

2 Sorry, _____ right or left at Circular Quay?

3 And then what _____ ?

**Conversation 2**

4 Excuse me, is Chinatown _____ ?

5 Am I _____ we go straight down this road first?

6 **Wei:** _____ second right into Kent Street, then third right.

**Pippa:** You _____ .

### Speaking

1 Look at the map of downtown Sydney on page 87. Draw an **✗** on the page and then explain to your teacher how to get there from the Sydney Opera House. Repeat the process, checking as many routes as you can using the language from Expressions.

### Language box

We use *be supposed to* or *be meant to* when we are talking about following instructions:

> I think we're supposed to turn left here.

> Weren't we meant to cross over the river?

These verbs can also refer to following or not following rules:

> You're meant to wait until the light is green, but nobody does.

> You're not supposed to park here, but I'm going to anyway.

Or to what somebody intended:

> I can't read his writing – is that word supposed to be 'stones' or 'stores'?

> That drawing's meant to be Sydney Opera House, is it?

travel

## Hint

When you give directions, use the imperative or the present simple. Don't use **please**.
**Take the next left.**
**You take the next left.**
~~Please take the next left.~~

## Hint

When we talk about directions, it is more normal to use **get to** than **arrive at**:
**Could you tell me how to get to the art gallery, please?**
**It'll take about twenty minutes to get to LA.**

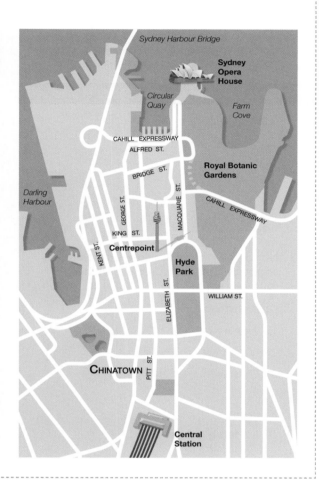

## Writing

**1** You are visiting a business colleague in Palermo, Sicily. They have given directions of how to get to their house from the airport, but you did not understand everything in the conversation. Send your colleague an email checking the following information:

• get bus from airport to the railway station / the port?
• walk down Via Maqueda / Via Roma?
• turn left / right down Corso Vittorio Emanuele?
• the house is near the church called Sant'Agostino / San Cataldo / San Nicolo?

**2** Write a short description of how you or someone you know had a difficulty with the directions someone had given them.

### Or to what people say:

There are supposed to be some great restaurants around here.

I thought you were meant to be able to speak the language! (= you said you could, but in fact you can't)

## Look

Look again at listening scripts 42.1 and 42.2 on page 127. Find more examples of *be supposed to* and *be meant to*.

## Lesson record

3 new words
from this lesson

1 ...........................
2 ...........................
3 ...........................

3 useful phrases
from this lesson

1 ...........................................
2 ...........................................
3 ...........................................

Things to remember

..................................................................
..................................................................
..................................................................
..................................................................
..................................................................
..................................................................

# How to **eat out**

**43**

## In this lesson you will learn useful phrases for discussing and ordering food.

### Starter

1 Which restaurants do you choose to go to in your country when you are with visitors? Why?

2 When you are abroad, how do you decide where to eat? How adventurous are you when it comes to eating local specialities?

### Expressions

43.1

1 Listen to two conversations. For each one, decide what sort of restaurant the people are in and what the people choose to eat.

| | | Type of restaurant | Choice of meal |
|---|---|---|---|
| 1 | Carlos | | |
| | Bill | | |
| 2 | Eva | | |
| | Amy | | |

2 Now listen again. This time complete the spaces with the words used on the recording.

Conversation 1

1 Well, there's _____ not far from here.

2 Otherwise, we could be _____ .

3 I think _____ one of the lamb dishes.

### Speaking

1 You are having dinner with a visitor. They have asked to try something local. Describe two dishes from the menu.

2 Think of two or three restaurants abroad, or away from your own town, that you particularly like. Describe them to your teacher. Include any details about the decor, atmosphere, specialities on the menu, etc., and / or the service there that make these restaurants special for you.

### Language box

To describe accurately how food is cooked, the following verbs are used:

| | |
|---|---|
| baked | cooked in the oven (used for cakes, bread, etc.) |
| boiled | cooked in very hot water |
| broiled | (AmE) grilled / barbecued |
| fried | cooked in oil on top of the cooker |
| grilled | cooked under a strong heat |
| roast | cooked in the oven, usually with a little oil (used for meats and vegetables) |
| steamed | cooked over water |

travel

## Hint

Some common adjectives for food and drink:
**savoury** – **sweet** (food)
**hot, spicy** – **mild** (curry dishes)
**rich, heavy** – **light** (dishes)
**still** – **sparkling, fizzy** (mineral water)

### Conversation 2

4   Well, you _____ the
    Greek vegetable dish ...

5   Well that sounds very nice. And
    _____ ?

6   No, _____ , thanks.

7   Well that was really good.
    _____ ?

8   No, no, I insist. _____ !

## Writing

1   **Read the following situations, and for each one write an email in response.**

    1   You have just been interviewed on the phone for a magazine about your business travels. They have now emailed to ask for some stories about your experiences of eating out abroad.

    2   A foreign client has emailed you, asking for advice on where to eat in your city when he arrives next month. Give him two or three choices, with reasons. For each restaurant explain:

        • type of food
        • your favourite dish
        • cost per person.

**Other expressions:**
It's served with ... / made from ...
It's a mixture of ... and ...
It comes with ...

## Look

Look again at listening script 43.1 on pages 127–128, and underline all the foods mentioned. Decide on all the different ways each of them can be cooked.

## Lesson record

| 3 new words from this lesson | 3 useful phrases from this lesson |
|---|---|
| 1 ................ | 1 ................................ |
| 2 ................ | 2 ................................ |
| 3 ................ | 3 ................................ |

Things to remember

...................................................................

...................................................................

...................................................................

...................................................................

...................................................................

...................................................................

# How to **ride in taxis**

**44**

**In this lesson you will learn useful phrases for travelling in taxis.**

## Starter

1 Which piece of advice 1–3 belongs to which place a–c?

a New York City

b Morocco

c Japan

1 You are expected to share a taxi with up to five others. If you are a single female, you will probably sit in the front.

2 The door of the taxi will open and close automatically. Pay the amount shown on the meter. No tip is necessary.

3 The lights on the top of the taxi tell you if the car is free. When only the middle is lit, the car is free. When all the lights are lit, the driver is off-duty. When no lights are on, the car is busy.

2 What is your experience of taking taxis in different countries?

## Speaking

1 Role-play the following conversations.

1 Choose a place in your town you are familiar with. Phone for a taxi (your teacher!) to get you there for a meeting in half an hour.

2 The taxi arrives. Tell the driver where you want to go. Remember to get a receipt.

3 Now choose a second destination. The taxi has no meter, so you will need to check the price before getting in.

travel

## Expressions

**1** Listen to two conversations relating to a taxi journey and answer the questions below.

   **1** What is the address of the person ordering the taxi?

   **2** Where does the person want to go to?

   **3** Does the taxi driver know how to get to the destination?

**2** Now listen again. This time complete the spaces with the words used by the client.

   **1** Hello. _____ please.

   **2** It'll be about twenty minutes _____ , I'm afraid.

   **3** **Driver:** Mr Hansen?

      **Mr Hansen:** Yes, that's right. _____ the Oasis Restaurant.

   **4** Right. Um, you can _____ if you like.

   **5** Could I _____ please?

   **6** Oh, and er, keep _____ .

## Writing

**1** You took two taxis yesterday with City Cabs. You left your umbrella in one of the taxis, but cannot remember which. You have phoned the taxi company, who have asked you to send them an email describing the trips you made to help them find the umbrella.

**2** A client is arriving from abroad and will need to get to your offices. Write an email to explain the best route for them to take in terms of price, time, and comfort, as well as the best form of transport.

## Language box

We often use these phrases when we are not sure of an exact location:

It's **just south of** the station.

It's **on this side of** the river **towards** the park.

I think it's **somewhere near** the post office.

It's **right in** the city centre.

It's **a little way out of** the centre, **in the direction of** the airport.

You'll see it **just after** the church.

It's **not too far from** the conference centre.

It's **just a few hundred metres along** this road.

## Look

Look again at listening script 44.1 on page 128. Find more examples of these phrases.

1 You are going to read about some typical methods by which tourists are cheated while they are on holiday. Read the extracts and match a title to each one.

A The airport scanner set-up

B The fake policeman routine

C The disgusting substance scam

D The crooked currency exchange

E The train compartment trick

2 Answer the question with the correct paragraph number. Which scam:

i happens when you are trying to save money? _____

ii involves a person in authority? _____

iii happens before you board your plane? _____

iv occurs because you leave your bags unattended? _____

v involves someone pretending to help you?

3 Find the words in the text that match the following definitions a–j.

a money and expensive possessions

b a machine which moves things along automatically

c suddenly starts making a loud sound

d very happy

e an unofficial system for doing business

f with no value

g to escape on foot

h knocks gently with the ends of fingers

i comes towards you

j gives something to someone

# Travel scams

So, you arrive at your holiday destination, looking forward to a stress-free fortnight away from it all, but no sooner do you get off the plane than you're tricked out of $200 of your spending money. That's what happened to me, anyway, and I'll tell you how. I took a taxi to my hotel, as everything was looking a little strange. When we stopped, I gave the driver a $100 bill, but he waved it in my face saying I'd confused it with a $1 note. So I gave him another bill, and while I was thanking him for pointing out my mistake, he drove off. It wasn't until I got to my hotel room that I realized he'd somehow pocketed my first $100 bill and got me to give him another one. As simple as that. But the taxi dodge is only one of the many travel scams used to relieve tourists of their money and belongings. Here are five more common scams to watch out for when you're far away from home:

1 _____

You're walking down the street, enjoying a bit of the local culture and admiring the architecture, when, splat! A large piece of what looks like bird poo lands on your shoulders, dirtying your best holiday clothes.

Suddenly a person appears with a cloth and offers to wipe off the mess, complaining about the pigeons that live in their city. Beware. While cleaning you up, they will also be robbing you of all the valuables in your pockets.

2 _____

You're at the airport and you put your laptop on the luggage scanner conveyor belt before waiting behind two people to go through the metal detector. The first

passes with no problems, but the detector goes off when the second person goes through. They then proceed to remove all their jewellery and empty their pockets of everything from coins to chewing gum. By the time you get through the machine the first person has disappeared, and so has your laptop.

**3** _____

You're delighted to find that changing your money on the black market from the suspicious-looking guy on the corner will give you a much better rate than at the bureau de change or the hotel front desk, and there's no commission either. You hand over your cash to get a huge number of notes, which you rush to put away before someone can take them. Counting your money in the hotel room, you realize you've been handed a pile of worthless notes.

*no sooner do you get off the plane than you're tricked out of $200*

**4** _____

There you are feeling very pleased with yourself for managing to find an empty compartment. While waiting for your train to leave the station, someone on the platform taps at the window calling to you. You go to find them, only to see them run off. When you return to your seat, you find an even emptier compartment – your bags have been stolen.

**5** _____

A friendly stranger starts talking to you and while you're chatting away, a policeman approaches. He says he's looking for some false banknotes and asks to see your passport and money. The other traveller hands his over and gets them back. When you hand over your cash, the policeman and the traveller disappear with it.

source: The Observer Sunday 1 September 2002
Escape: Travel scams

knife used by doctors performing operations

**scam** /skæm/ a trick which is designed to take money from people in a dishonest way

**scamp** /skæmp/ a child who enjoys playing tricks and causing trouble: *that little scamp has hidden my*

# reading bank

**1** You are going to read about recent trends in the use of mobile phones. Read the first three paragraphs quickly (to … 'Most young children will use their thumbs'). Then decide if the following statements are true (T) or false (F).

1 A quarter of British people spend 20% of their day on their mobile phone. _____

2 33% of people say that they have used their mobile in the bathroom. _____

3 The nineteen-year-old British girl sent more text messages per month than the Danish man. _____

4 The Danish man's mobile phone bill went up five times. _____

5 The British girl gave up going to classes at college because she couldn't use her mobile. _____

6 Most children use their mobile to speak to their friends and to play games. _____

7 Children use their thumbs to operate their mobiles because this finger is the strongest. _____

**2** Read the second half of the text to the end, and answer the following questions.

1 How do the mobile phone companies target young children?

2 How has the number of young mobile users changed in the last few years?

3 What trends can be seen in the spending habits of teenagers and under-25s?

4 What does the author think will happen in the future?

**3** Find the words in the text that match the following definitions 1–8.

1 A small device – this is a word sometimes used when you don't know the correct name (paragraph two).

_____

2 The treatment that ill people receive to help them recover (paragraph two).

_____

3 When something is too expensive for your budget or possibilities (paragraph two).

_____

4 To send a written message on your mobile (paragraph three).

_____

5 Things used to attract the interest of potential buyers and to promote sales (paragraph four).

_____

6 The sound that your mobile makes when someone calls you (paragraph four).

_____

7 The money you can spend after you have paid for essential items (paragraph five).

_____

8 Extra components that you can buy to add to another device (paragraph six).

_____

**4** From having read the article, who do you think might say the following? Choose one of the people from the box. The sentences do not appear in the text.

| a doctor   a teacher   a parent |
|---|
| an eighteen-year-old girl   a young boy |

1 'I like the new games and I send lots of messages to my friends.'

2 'She was suffering from depression and needed treatment seriously.'

3 'I gave him one when he was eight because I wanted to be able to contact him at all times.'

4 'I'm in constant touch with all my friends and I use it for my diary as well.'

5 'I make them turn them off before they come in.'

# MOBILE MADNESS

'I went to the opera the other night to watch 'Madam Butterfly' and just as she was about to kill herself, with the knife above her head, a mobile phone started to ring somewhere in the opera house.'

British people seem to have gone 'mobile mad'. 20% of British people spend an astonishing quarter of their day on mobile phones. We have become so obsessed with the little gadget that we can't leave our

## "I only feel happy when I hear my mobile beeping"

house without it! One in three people confess to having used their mobile in the bathroom! The question of mobile telephone addiction is now being taken seriously in many countries. Special clinics are now offering therapy to people who cannot live without their mobile. A Scandinavian driver had to receive treatment in a specialized clinic for his addiction to SMS texting (short message services). The twenty-five-year-old worked nights and spent his daylight hours sending an average of 217 text messages per day. His quarterly mobile phone bill quintupled to 12,000 crowns (£967) – unaffordable on his Danish driver's salary. In Britain, a nineteen-year-old girl asked for help because she would rather spend money on pay-and-go vouchers for her mobile than on food or clothes. She admits to sending around 1,600 text messages a month. 'I only feel happy when I hear my mobile beeping. When I don't have any credit left I become depressed. I need to check my mobile every two minutes. I stopped going to classes at college because I couldn't answer my phone'.

## 33% of children between the ages of ten and fourteen now have their own mobile

## YOUNG USERS

Over half of children with mobiles prefer to text rather than chat to stay in touch, and there is one report that claims that the thumbs of young children are getting bigger and stronger because they spend so much time texting and playing computer games. It is true that children use their thumbs more than adults nowadays. Adults use their index finger to dial or text, press the button in the lift, key in information on the computer or calculator and so on, but most young children will use their thumbs.

The mobile phone industry claims that it does not target the under-sixteens. But it is true that the adult market is beginning to slow down. OFTEL, the industry regulator in the UK, maintains that three quarters of the adult British population now own a mobile phone. To increase sales of mobile phones to the younger age groups, mobile phone companies have created a range of gimmicks to attract young children – fancy ringtones using the latest pop songs, screensavers using popular cartoon figures such as Harry Potter, Spiderman, and even Winnie the Pooh. Many companies now offer short videos, photographs, even online jokes! Not surprisingly, the number of very young mobile users, between the ages of five and nine, has jumped from 80,000 in 2000 to nearly 1,000,000 now. 33% of children between the ages of ten and fourteen now have their own mobile.

## MUSIC OR MOBILE?

Young people used to spend large amounts of money on music, but the latest studies reveal that people under the age of twenty-five now spend five times more money on mobile phones than they do on music. A recent study found that this age group annually spends £3 billion of its disposable income on mobile handsets, calls, and data, compared with just £600 million on CDs and other music formats. Under-25s are spending £107 million on mobile music in the UK each year, equivalent to 75 million ringtone downloads. In contrast, music industry figures indicate that CD single sales have fallen '30 to 50%' during the same period.

Mobile phones and accessories account for almost 11% of British under-25s' spending. On average people in this age group spend £238 on their mobile phone compared to only £49 on music.

With the constant advances in mobile telephony, these figures can only increase.

source: CBBC NEWSROUND 12/7/05
http://news.bbc.co.uk(cbbcnews/hi/sci_tech/
newsid_1892000/1892881.stm
www.mobile.be/news_article.php?page=236

# reading bank

**03**

**1** You are going to read about a food scandal in Hungary. Read the article and match a title to each paragraph A-D.

1 How paprika is used
2 The scandal
3 The outcome
4 Where and how paprika is grown

**2** Answer the following multiple choice questions, according to the article.

1 Why is paprika so important to Hungarians?
   a It is only grown in Hungary.
   b It is very expensive.
   c It is used in the cooking of almost every main dish.

2 Why did the ban cause such a problem?
   a Because people didn't know what to use in cooking instead of paprika.
   b Because people were scared of dying.
   c Because people had too much paprika on their shelves at home.

3 How did the poison get into the paprika?
   a Foreign growers mixed mushrooms with the paprika.
   b Some producers mixed cheaper paprika from abroad with local paprika.
   c It was mixed abroad, with other products.

4 Why are some types of paprika spicier?
   a More seeds are included in the powder.
   b Spices from other countries are mixed into the powder.
   c The powder is manufactured at higher temperatures.

5 How did the authorities find out who was responsible?
   a They interviewed key producers.
   b They searched all paprika products.
   c They took all stocks off the supermarket shelves.

6 Where is paprika grown?
   a In the middle of the country.
   b In southern Hungary.
   c All over the country.

7 Where can tourists find out about paprika, and taste it?
   a In Szeged and Kalocsa.
   b At the paprika museum in Budapest.
   c At festivals all over Hungary.

8 For how long was it not possible to buy paprika in Hungary?
   a Eight months.
   b Two months.
   c Two weeks.

**3** Match the words (1-7) with the definitions (a-g).

1 arouse
2 contaminated
3 crush
4 harmless
5 ingredient
6 under threat
7 sewage

a made dirty or poisoned by the addition of a chemical
b in danger
c waste substances removed from toilets through underground pipes
d one of the foods or liquids that you use in making a meal
e to cause a particular emotion or attitude
f to press something very hard so that it breaks into pieces
g not at all dangerous

# Paprika panic

If it's about paprika, it's news in Hungary. The national spice, paprika, is a key ingredient in most Hungarian meat dishes – and in some, the main ingredient. Life is unimaginable without it: you'll find matching salt, pepper, and paprika shakers on every restaurant table, and in the home. Apart from politics, there are few subjects that can arouse such strong feelings in Hungarians as the subject of how to cook with paprika.

### A

But on Thursday 28th October the worst happened: Hungary woke up to hear that the government had banned the sale of the spice. It was announced that the paprika in shops and even their own kitchens, and on dining tables throughout the country, may contain poison. Not only was the problem of what to cook and eat a worry, but there was also the risk of becoming ill.

The moment the news broke, the leading opposition party called for an investigation into the scandal. Two months previously, sixty tons of imported paprika, contaminated with a poisonous fungus called aflatoxin, had been discovered, but apparently no action had been taken. Meanwhile, some producers had illegally mixed these cheaper varieties with their own local produce, to make up for a bad summer and poor pepper crops. Now, Hungary's market position as one of the world's leading paprika producers, with exports of over 5,000 tons of 'red gold' a year, worth around €13 million, was under threat.

### B

To the outside world, the word 'paprika' only refers to the rich red powder made from the dried *capsicum annuum L.* red pepper. In Hungary, however, 'paprika' also refers to their range of fresh peppers, which are eaten, cooked and stuffed, chopped raw and added to soups, or as an accompaniment to bread, cheese, and salami. Of the powdered form of paprika, the form that was banned, there is a 'sweet' variety, used to liven up soups and stews – such as the national dish, goulash – with its flavour and colour, and a 'hot' variety, typically sprinkled onto egg or potato salads for decoration, or used as a key ingredient in spicy red sausages.

### C

The 2,000 or so hours of sunshine which reach the Hungarian Great Plain each year are perfect for the cultivation of *capsicum annuum L.* As they mature, the peppers change from green to brown and finally to a rich red. Traditionally, these were dried in early autumn on long threads of string against the whitewashed walls of every house, to be stored when dry for crumbling into cooking.

Nowadays, however, the peppers are dried in factories and crushed to powder between stones and steel cylinders. The seeds of the pepper are added in varying quantities to determine the degree of spiciness of the final product. Production is centred in the south of the country around the two 'paprika capitals' of Kalocsa, which has a week-long paprika festival every September as well as a paprika museum, and Szeged, where paprika production employs 3,000 people, and where you can visit the world's only paprika research laboratories.

So back in October, a vital part of Hungarian life was under threat. Thousands of worried citizens, frightened of illness, phoned the National Ambulance Service. Despite being told that the amount of poison was minimal and harmless, one mother told a newspaper that this was like asking people to drink bottled water containing 99% mineral water and 1% sewage.

### D

Eventually, after interviews with top paprika-producing executives, the Hungarian 'FBI' tracked down those responsible for the crisis. Two weeks on, government officials – desperate to restore consumer confidence in one of the country's most famous products as quickly as possible – stated that they believed they had the problem fully under control.

One by one, products containing paprika were tested. By early November, paprika products were slowly beginning to make their way back to the supermarket shelves. Finally, on a historic day, the ban on sales was lifted as paprika was given the all-clear. And not one person had been admitted to hospital!

Eight months later, a number of individuals were fined a total of €40,000 for misleading consumers, and, to ensure lasting safety for all housewives, the government enforced strict regulations on the industry concerning spot checks and product labelling.

So at last, Hungarians, whose economy, culture, and pride is represented and upheld by the red powder, could celebrate together over a kettle of goulash. As they say in Hungary: *One man may yearn for fame, another for wealth, but everyone yearns for paprika goulash.*

# reading bank

**1** You are going to read about the development of international trade during the Renaissance period. Read the text below and put these sentences a–e back into the text in the best place 1–5.

a They had learnt all of this from eastern cultures.

b In the same way, the word 'algebra' was adopted from the Arabic word for restoration, 'al-jabru'.

c Payment on goods was often in silver or gold, but as sales increased and more than two people became involved in any one business deal, new ways of trading were required.

d The financial reality was probably less simple than that.

e Hindu-Arabic numerals were much better because they allowed for complex and more abstract solutions to calculating profit and loss.

**2** Read the text again and mark the following true (T) or false (F).

1 The concept of 'zero' (0) was introduced into Europe in the twelfth century. _____

2 Fibonacci introduced the signs $+$, $-$, and X to Europe. _____

3 The word *cheque* has its origin in Hindi. _____

4 The prohibition on usury was obeyed by merchants of all cultures. _____

5 The Florentine Medici family began their political and economic career as bankers. _____

**3** Put the following events in the order that they happened 1–5, and then check your answers in the text.

a _____ Paper bills of exchange were first used to pay for goods in Europe.

b _____ Fibonacci started to explain Hindu-Arabic numerals to Europeans.

c _____ The city-state of Venice was making a profit of four million ducats a year.

d _____ Al-Khowârizmî wrote a book that included the rules of arithmetic for the decimal system.

e _____ The Medici Bank was set up in Florence, Italy.

**4** Match the words (1–7) with the definitions (a–g).

1 awkward
2 a balance sheet
3 to barter
4 creditworthiness
5 delivery
6 to handle
7 merchandise

a when goods arrive
b to deal with (something)
c goods that are traded
d difficult, not easy to use
e to exchange one object for another without using money
f a document showing money coming in and out of a company
g how much a company or bank trusts a client to pay money back

are often kept by human beings as pets or trained for work

**Doge** /dəʊdʒ/ the leader of Venice from the 8th to the 18th century

**dogfight** /dɒgfaɪt/ a fight between aircraft in which they fly around close to each other

# When East met West

In 1423 the Doge of Venice gave a verbal balance sheet of the commercial state of his city. It gives some idea of the growing size and complexity of trade and finance in the early fifteenth century. He stated that 'Venetian exports to the whole world represent 10 million ducats a year; her imports amount to another ten million. On these twenty millions, she made a profit of four million, or interest at the rate of twenty per cent.'

**1**

Nevertheless, balancing the import and export of international goods seems so familiar to us today that it is easy to forget that the Renaissance was the birthplace of modern capitalism. But it would be wrong to say that this was exclusively a European development. Just as European merchants bought and sold in the exotic markets of the east, they also began to use Arabic ways of doing business through their contact with the trading centres of North Africa and the Middle East.

At the beginning of the thirteenth century, a merchant from Pisa called Fibonacci wrote a series of influential books on mathematics, using his commercial experience with Arabic ways of calculating profit and loss. In 1202 he completed his study of mathematics and calculation entitled *Liber abbaci*, based on his time working in Algeria using Hindu-Arabic numerals. In his commercial exchanges with Arab merchants in the eastern bazaars, Fibonacci realized that the European practice of using Roman numerals and the abacus was awkward and time-consuming.

**2**

So Fibonacci carefully explained the nature of the Hindu-Arabic numerals from 0 to 9, as well as the use of the decimal point. He also used them in solving commercial problems, such as deciding on weights and measurements, bartering, and charging interest. If this seems elementary today, we should remember that the signs for addition, subtraction, and multiplication were unknown in Europe before Fibonacci.

The Arabic commercial practice that Fibonacci copied came from much earlier Arabic developments in mathematics and geometry. Around AD 825 the Persian astronomer al-Khowârizmî had written a book that included the rules of arithmetic for the decimal system, and his Latinized name provided the foundation of modern mathematics: the algorithm.

**3**

Fibonacci's new methods were gradually adopted in the trading centres of Venice, Florence, and Genoa, as Italian merchants realized that new ways of keeping records of more complex and international transactions were needed.

**4**

One of the most significant innovations was the bill of exchange, which was the earliest form of paper money. This was the ancestor of the modern cheque, which originated from the medieval Arabic 'sakk'. When you write a cheque, you draw on your creditworthiness at a bank. Your bank will honour the cheque when the holder presents it for payment. Similarly, by 1350 Italian traders were paying for merchandise with a paper bill of exchange drawn from a powerful merchant family. This bill would be paid when presented on a specific date, or upon delivery of the goods. Merchant families that guaranteed these transactions on pieces of paper became bankers as well as merchants.

The banker made money on these transactions by charging interest based on the time it took for the bill to be repaid, and by manipulating exchange rates.

Both medieval Christianity and Islam prohibited the charging of interest on a loan, called *usury*. In practice, both cultures found ways to avoid this problem in order to maximize profit. Merchant bankers could hide the interest by 'officially' lending money in one currency and then collecting it in a different one. The merchant made his profit by using a favourable rate of exchange that gave him a percentage of the original amount. Another solution was to employ Jewish merchants to handle credit transactions, as their religion had no prohibition against usury.

The accumulating wealth and status of the merchant bankers was the basis for the political power and artistic development of the Renaissance. The famous Medici family, who dominated culture and politics in Florence during the fifteenth century, began as merchant bankers. In 1397 Giovanni de Bicci de' Medici established the Medici Bank in Florence, which perfected the art of accounting, deposit banking, maritime insurance, and the use of bills of exchange.

**5**

It was trade and exchange with the east, and the adoption of these more systematic ways of doing business that created the conditions for Renaissance art, culture, and consumption.

# listening bank

## Modding

You are going to listen to a radio interview about the art of rebuilding and adapting computers, known as *modding*. The speakers use the term *mod* for a modified computer and *modder* for the person who carries out the modification.

You will hear two guests, Dirk Stein and Todd Buckingham, being interviewed about modding. Listen to the interview as many times as you like, and try to answer the questions below.

The recording is on the MultiROM at the back of this Student's Book.

**1** Mark the sentences below about the interviews true (T) or false (F).

1 Modders always base their designs on mods made by other people. _____

2 One modder has a computer that serves coffee. _____

3 Making a computer run faster can make it overheat. _____

4 To enter the case mod contest you have to send your mod to the competition organizers. _____

5 The TIE fighter mod won the fantasy mod contest. _____

6 Modding has become popular because computer manufacturers are not producing what users want. _____

7 Todd believes that all the current computer manufacturers will continue into the next decade. _____

**2** Listen to the interviews with Dirk and Todd again and answer the questions below.

1 What is the origin of the term 'modding'?

_____

2 What was the problem with adding a fan to a computer?

_____

3 Why does Dirk refuse to tell the interviewer his modding idea?

_____

4 What prize was awarded to the last winners of the modding competition?

_____

**3** Match each beginning of a sentence (1–8) to an ending (a–h). All the words are in the listening script.

1 The 'brain' of the computer is the _____

2 The pilot sits in the _____

3 You need your _____

4 You can carry a _____

5 A personal computer, or _____

6 Computer components are usually housed in a _____

7 If a machine _____

8 If something is state-of-the-art, _____

a cockpit of a plane.

b CPU, a powerful microprocessor.

c it has the most up-to-date, modern design.

d case made of metal or plastic.

e laptop around if you need to work when you're travelling.

f PC, is a computer you can use on a desk.

g toolbox when you have to repair something.

h overheats, it gets too hot.

The listening script for this recording is on pages 128–129.

# listening bank

## Downshifting

You are going to listen to a radio interview about people who leave their stressful professional lives in the city in favour of a quieter and less prosperous lifestyle in the country. The speakers refer to the people involved as *downshifters* and to the trend in general as *downshifting*. Listen to the interview as many times as you like, and try to answer the questions below.

The recording is on the MultiROM at the back of this Student's Book.

1 Listen to the interview and tick (✓) the type of people who can be described as downshifters.

a A university graduate who wants to drop out of society. _____

b A couple who buy a new car every year. _____

c A family who value their free time more than the things they own. _____

d A 55-year-old who now works seven hours instead of eleven hours a day. _____

e A redundant engineer who now runs a village bakery. _____

f A mother who has taken on more hours to be financially independent. _____

g A divorced parent who now works only part-time. _____

h An ex-lawyer who now writes and illustrates children's stories. _____

2 Listen again and (circle) the best answer.

1 Downshifters generally have:
   a less money and more stability.
   b less money and less stability.
   c less money and no stability.

2 According to Dr Schwarz, how many groups of people does downshifting appeal to?
   a Two.
   b Three.
   c Four.

3 The main reason why downshifters decide to change their lives is because:
   a they want to spend more time with their family.
   b their marriage has broken up.
   c they want a healthier lifestyle.

4 The most common problem downshifters face in the first year is:
   a getting used to living in a smaller space.

b stress caused by spending more time with their partner.

c not having enough money while building their business.

5 Helena decided to downshift because:
   a she didn't get on with her colleagues.
   b she wanted more time to learn about dogs.
   c she didn't have any job satisfaction any more.

6 Before downshifting, Helena recommends that you should:
   a get to know about a new country if you are moving abroad.
   b get to know the area that you are moving to.
   c make sure you choose a place in the country to move to.

7 Helena now works with dog owners whose dogs:
   a have behavioural problems.
   b have a serious illness.
   c do not get enough exercise.

The listening script for this recording is on pages 129–130.

Answer key
1 c, d, e, g, h
2 1 b
  2 b
  3 a
  4 c
  5 c
  6 b
  7 a

business one : one          101

# listening bank

## Fishy business

You are going to listen to an interview with Ian Middlehurst, who runs a small business selling fish, meat, and other produce just outside Manchester, England. Listen to the interview as many times as you like, and try to answer the questions below.

The recording is on the MultiROM at the back of this Student's Book.

**1** Listen to the interview, and put the following events in the order (1–5) that they happened.

a _____ Ian's uncle retired.

b _____ His father was made redundant.

c _____ Another fish shop opened down the road.

d _____ His father and uncle bought the shop.

e _____ His father only looked after the fish.

**2** Listen and write down where Ian sources the following food products.

1 Most of the fish. _____

2 Tuna and swordfish. _____

3 Rabbits and pigeons. _____

4 Venison and chicken. _____

**3** Look at the sentences below about the shop and mark them true (T) or false (F), according to the recording.

1 Staff at the shop will cook seafood for the customers. _____

2 The shop will lend customers equipment for cooking. _____

3 The new supermarket was a disaster for Ian's business. _____

4 The staff will cook food for customers based on recipes they bring to the shop. _____

5 The shop delivers fresh produce to customers. _____

6 Over the years the shop has improved by installing air-conditioning. _____

7 The shop only uses special advertising at Christmas. _____

**4** Listen again to the end of the recording and tick (✓) the ways that customers hear about the shop.

- TV adverts
- Adverts in magazines
- Cooking and food websites
- Posters
- Door-to-door mailings
- Word of mouth

The listening script for this recording is on page 130.

## eBay

**04**

You are going to listen to an interview about the successful online business eBay. Listen to the interview as many times as you like, and try to answer the questions below.

The recording is on the MultiROM at the back of this Student's Book.

**1** What do these numbers refer to in the recording?

30%

400,000

1995

10%

50 million

$3,000

147 million

€9

**2** Who are the following people?

Jack Wallace

Pierre Omidyar

Meg Whitman

**3** Look at the sentences below about eBay and mark the sentences true (T) or false (F) according to the recording.

1 It took about two years for eBay to become popular. _____

2 British people spend more money on eBay than on the cinema. _____

3 Many traditional shops use eBay as another way to sell their goods. _____

4 Most of the articles on eBay are brand new. _____

5 The real strength of eBay is the low cost of the items on sale. _____

6 There are 3 billion eBay users. _____

7 If you open a shop on eBay, the first month costs nothing. _____

**4** Listen again, and answer these questions about the interview.

1 Jack Wallace says we have lots of things in our houses that we never use. What three examples does he give?

2 What is PayPal?

3 The number of cases of fraud on eBay is very low. How does Pierre Omidyar explain this?

4 How does the eBay Feedback System work?

5 As well as paying a daily fee, what other payment do shops on eBay have to pay?

The listening script for this recording is on pages 130–132.

**Answer key**

1 30%: the operating profit margins of eBay
400,000: the number of people who earn all or at least part of their annual income through eBay
1995: the year eBay was founded
10%: of all the time that British people spend on the Internet is spent on eBay
50 million: number of different items on offer
$3,000: the value of goods in an average house that are not used
147 million: number of registered eBay users
€9: the daily cost of maintaining a shop on eBay

2 Jack Wallace: Internet and e-commerce expert, B2B Consultants, New York
Pierre Omidyar: founder of eBay
Meg Whitman: eBay's CEO

3 1 F (eBay was popular within the first six months)
2 T
3 T
4 F ('there are more second-hand items for sale')
5 F ('the real strength of eBay is the very professional management team that run the company')
6 F (this is the number of feedback comments)
7 T ('the first thirty days are completely free')

4 1 That old computer, the camping equipment that we never use now, a present that somebody gave us and we don't really want.
2 It's a secure system of paying for things by credit card online.
3 Because he thinks people are honest.
4 When you buy or sell something on eBay you leave a feedback comment on the other person. You can check these comments before you do business with a person.
5 They have to pay a small commission on goods sold.

# listening bank

## Spanish weddings

You are going to listen to an interview with Gemma Sala, who is talking about a wedding company in Spain, called D'Elite Spain Wedding, which she set up with her partner Gianna Soria. Listen to the interview as many times as you like, and try to answer the questions below.

The recording is on the MultiROM at the back of this Student's Book.

**1** Look at the sentences below about the interview and mark them true (T) or false (F).

1 It's important for the wedding planner to be there on the day of the wedding. ____

2 Spanish weddings tend to be large and expensive, even if the family haven't got much money. ____

3 The couple often help to solve problems on the day of the wedding. ____

4 The happiest part is seeing the smiling faces on the photos afterwards. ____

best man

groom

bride

lapel

bouquet

buttonhole

**2** Listen again, and answer these questions about the interview.

1 What percentage of her weddings are in the Barcelona region?

2 Do couples always contract a photographer?

3 How long has the company been going?

4 Who does the bride give her bouquet to when the music stops?

5 What do Gemma and her partner always carry in case there are last-minute problems?

6 Why did the hired coach driver once wait in the wrong place?

7 What three qualities does Gemma say a wedding planner should have?

8 What should the bride and groom find time to do?

9 What two things are essential for a happy marriage, according to Gemma?

**3** Match the words from the interview 1–6 with the correct definition a–f.

1 to set up ____

2 to foresee a problem ____

3 to sort something out ____

4 a slip-up ____

5 to turn out well ____

6 chaotic ____

a a mistake

b completely disorganized

c to realize that a problem could happen, and make plans to deal with it

d to be OK in the end

e to start a company / organization

f to solve a problem

The listening script for this recording is on pages 132–133.

# listening bank

## The Edinburgh International Festival

You are going to listen to an interview with Nicky Pritchett-Brown, Sponsorship and Development Director of the Edinburgh International Festival. Listen to the interview as many times as you like, and try to answer the questions below.

The recording is on the MultiROM at the back of this Student's Book.

**1** Look at the incorrect sentences below. Listen to Nicky and correct the sentences.

1 There are performances of opera, dance, and drama only.

2 The festival started in 1974.

3 The festival is for Scottish artists and performers only.

4 Ticket prices are high, so only rich people can afford to go.

5 The box office revenues provide enough money to pay for the festival.

6 All companies have a sponsorship budget.

7 Companies are happy to sponsor any event.

**2** Look at the sentences below about the interview and mark them true (T) or false (F).

1 Nicky's job is to raise money from public sector funds. _____

2 Nicky believes the Festival is important for Scotland's economy. _____

3 Nicky holds events throughout the year to keep sponsors informed. _____

4 Sponsorship ranges from £500 to limitless amounts for a complete series of events. _____

5 Nicky thinks that the people living and working in Edinburgh like having the festival. _____

**3** Listen again, and answer these questions about the sponsorship of the festival.

1 Apart from advertising for the company, what other benefits do companies get when they sponsor an event?

2 In the past, it was popular for companies to sponsor events so that they could take their own clients to performances. What is this called?

3 Some events are considered to be risky to sponsor. What sort of events are these?

4 According to Nicky, why do Standard Life like to sponsor contemporary events?

**4** What is the relationship of the following companies to the festival?

Bank of Scotland

Renault

Scottish and Newcastle

The listening script for this recording is on pages 133–134.

## Answer key

1 1 There are also classical solo and orchestral concerts.
2 In 1947.
3 It's very international (performers, productions, audience).
4 Ticket prices are 'significantly cheaper' than at other festivals.
5 Box office is not enough: without corporate sponsorship the festival would not take place.
6 Some companies sponsor the Festival with money from their Marketing or Corporate Social Responsibility budget, rather than a sponsorship budget.
7 There is careful discussion to make sure that the event and a company wishing to sponsor it are suitably matched. Other companies want something more traditional, and therefore less risky.

2 1 F (From private sector funds.)
2 T
3 T
4 F
5 F

3 1 A package of tickets, an association with excellence, and investment in the community.
2 Corporate Entertainment.
3 Performances with nudity, bad language, or 'difficult' topics.
4 To keep their image up-to-date.

4 The Bank of Scotland have sponsored the Festival since it began in 1947.
Renault Espace lend cars for the festival to ferry people around.
Scottish and Newcastle's headquarters are in Edinburgh, so it is important that new foreign clients see Edinburgh as an international city.

# listening bank

## The call centre

You are going to listen to an interview about Delta Call Centre Services and its new building design. Listen to the interview as many times as you like, and try to answer the questions below.

The recording is on the MultiROM at the back of this Student's Book.

**1** Read the following summary of the recording about Delta Call Centre Services. There are five mistakes in the information. Find and correct these mistakes.

> Delta changed its offices in 1996. These new premises were necessary because the company wanted a different image to present to its clients. The building has three floors with a large social area on the ground floor. Staff at Delta are much happier with the facilities of the new building and the company says that they are now more productive. Most employees at Delta are between 35 and 45 years old. The building cost more than 10 million pounds to build, but the management thinks it was a good investment.

**2** Michael Burton, personnel manager of Delta, mentions the following numbers at the beginning of the recording. What do these numbers refer to?

150

60%

3 to 400

5%

250

**3** Four people speak in this recording: Michael Burton (personnel manager), Susan Hartley (the architect), Jennifer (an employee), and the interviewer of the programme. Who do you think makes the following statements? Mark your answers and then listen to see if you were correct.

1 'It makes them feel good about working there.' ............

2 'It's easier now to change round the people in the teams more frequently.' ............

3 'I think the main reason was the high level of stress that the job has.' ............

4 'So it was felt that the solution was to design and build new offices.' ............

5 'They can all see each other, but it doesn't feel crowded at all.' ............

6 'But for the ordinary worker, the job is still the same, and that can be stressful.' ............

7 'We even spend a lot of time here after work'. ............

8 'It's important to give a positive and cheerful image when you're working.' ............

9 'It seems to have been money very well spent.' ............

The listening script for this recording is on pages 134–135.

# listening bank

## Bill Newson, a New Zealand trade-union manager

You are going to listen to an interview with Bill Newson, a New Zealander who works as The Assistant Operations Director for the New Zealand Engineering, Printing, and Manufacturing Union. Listen to the interview as many times as you like, and try to answer the questions below.

The recording is on the MultiROM at the back of this Student's Book.

**1** Listen to the first part of the interview with Bill. Look at the sentences below and mark them true (T) or false (F) according to the recording.

1 12% of New Zealand workers are members of unions. _____

2 There are about thirteen field workers in his team. _____

3 His contact with the field workers is usually not face-to-face. _____

4 The New Zealand economy is depressed at the moment. _____

5 The unions hope to achieve a better pay increase this year than in recent years. _____

6 Soon they'll start negotiating with employers' associations. _____

7 He expects negotiations with the employers' associations to be difficult. _____

8 Personal development of people in his team is very important for him. _____

**2** In the second part of the interview, Bill gives a case study of a problem he has solved. Listen and complete the sentences below.

1 I try to work it out by thinking about the different parts of the issue and setting up what I call _____ .

2 So I can try to satisfy at least some of the employer's needs _____ the things that are important to us.

3 In bargaining for a collective agreement, an engineering company wanted to

   _____ .

4 We found out that this employer had recently _____ in a very specialized area of work, because the contract was given to a lower-priced competitor.

5 We agreed that the employer _____ this specific type of specialized work, against this specific competing company, _____ no extra overtime pay.

6 One year later we _____ , but within two years the employer had won enough work to prove that his company provided better quality.

**3** In the third part of the interview, Bill gives a case study of a problem where the workers found a solution. Listen to the third part of the interview, and answer the questions about the pictures below.

1 Look at the three pictures a–c and tick the picture that shows the phones' packaging before the workers' solution.

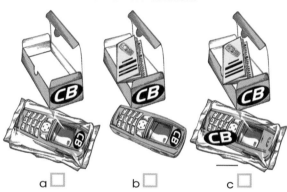

a ☐  b ☐  c ☐

2 Look at the three pictures d–f below and tick the picture which shows the phones' packaging after the workers' solution.

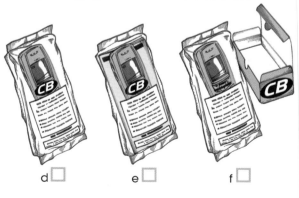

d ☐  e ☐  f ☐

The listening script for this recording is on pages 135–136.

# grammar bank

## The present

### Present simple (*I walk*)

The present simple is used for general facts about the present, descriptions, habits, routines, and schedules.

> Turkey has a population of around 72 million. (general fact)
> This new model looks very modern. (description)
> I start work at 7.30. (routine)
> The ferry leaves Milazzo at 8.00. (schedule)

The present simple is used for stative verbs. These are verbs used to describe ways of thinking, possession, and senses (*taste, hear, feel*, etc.).

> I don't like long meetings. (way of thinking)
> The parent company owns four subsidiaries. (possession)
> I like your velvet coat. It feels lovely. (sense)

### Present continuous (*I am walking*)

The present continuous is used to talk about actions at the time of speaking, actions happening around now, and temporary actions.

> He's eating lunch at the moment. (time of speaking)
> I'm working on a project in Lincoln for six months. (happening around now)
> The company is waiting for news of the takeover. (temporary actions)

It is also used to express irritation at an annoying situation that often happens.

> He's always working from home when I need to speak to him!

It is used to talk about the future to refer to definite future arrangements.

> I'm meeting Pekka from head office at three this afternoon.

### Present perfect (*I have walked*)

The present perfect is used for actions which took place in the past. But it is used to describe actions in unfinished time periods, or for actions that have very recently finished. It may be used to report news.

> I have worked here for fifteen years.
> (unfinished time period = fifteen years ago to now)
> We haven't heard any news.
> (unfinished time period = from start of waiting to now)
> Tom's been to Lisbon five times.
> (unfinished time period = Tom's entire life up to now)
> I've just sent the report! Now I can relax.
> (very recently finished)
> The managing director has resigned! (news)

The present perfect continuous (*I have been working*) is used in a similar way to the present perfect. It is preferred when we want to emphasize how long an action has taken.

> Andrea's been cycling around Chile for six months.

The present perfect continuous is often used to talk about a past action with a visible present result.

> He has been working non-stop for forty-eight hours and he looks like he'll fall asleep any minute.
> (past action = working non-stop, present result = he looks like he'll fall asleep)

## The past

### Past simple (*I walked*)

The past simple is used for actions that happened in finished time periods.

> I worked in La Coruña for five years in the 1980s.
> (finished time period = the 1980s)
> Kai spoke to the suppliers yesterday.
> (finished time period = yesterday)

### Past continuous (*I was walking*)

The past simple is the most common tense used for past actions. The past continuous is often used with the past simple to emphasize background information, and longer actions.

> When I arrived in Sweden, the wind was blowing and the snow was falling heavily. (= background information, weather)
> Fabio dropped all his papers while he was giving his presentation. (shorter action = dropped papers, longer action = was giving his presentation)

### Past perfect (*I had walked*)

The past simple is the most common tense used for past actions. The past perfect is used with the past simple to show earlier actions.

> When I got back to the room, I discovered he had left.

Often, however, the past simple is used in both cases.

> He was arrested after they discovered the theft.

There is also a past perfect continuous, used to emphasize the length of an action.

> They were tired because they had been working all day.

## The future

### Future simple (*I will walk*)

*Will* is used for general predictions about the future.

> The cost of rent will fall over the next ten years.

*Will* is often used in the present for offers and immediate decisions.

> The client has arrived early so I'll go downstairs and meet her. (= decide immediately to go downstairs)
> I know you have had arguments with Julia, so I'll phone her instead. (= offer to telephone Julia)

### *Going to* future (*I am going to walk*)

*Going to* and *will* can often be used in the same way to make predictions.

> The cost of rent is going to fall over the next ten years.

*Going to* is used in predictions which are based on present evidence.

> Because our suppliers are closing down, we're going to have difficulty getting new equipment. (present evidence = the suppliers are closing down, prediction = have difficulty getting new equipment)

Both *going to* and the present continuous are used to describe definite future arrangements.

> I'm going to meet Pekka from head office at three this afternoon.

## Future continuous (*I will be walking*)

We use the future continuous when we predict what will happen at a specified future time.

> Theresa will be leaving the office at six. (prediction = Theresa will be leaving the office, specified future time = at six)

It is often used to predict what people are doing at the time of speaking.

> Yvain isn't answering his mobile. Oh, I know why: he'll be driving to work now. (prediction = he'll be driving to work)

Like *going to* and the present continuous, the future continuous is used to talk about future plans and arrangements.

> The visitors from Pusan will be arriving at eleven tomorrow and then they'll be visiting the factory for the rest of the day. (plans and arrangements = arriving at eleven, visiting the factory)

## Future perfect (*I will have walked*)

The future perfect is used with other future tenses. It is used to show that an action happens before a specified future time.

> The project will have ended by the start of next week. (action happening before = the project will have ended, specified future time = the start of next week)

It is used to show that an action happens before another future event.

> They'll have sold all the tickets before the concert. (action happening before = they'll have sold all the tickets, future event = the concert)

There is also a future perfect continuous. This is used to emphasize the length of an action.

> By the launch date at the end of this year, we'll have been working on the project for eighteen months. (action happening before = we'll have been working on the project, future time = the launch date at the end of this year)

# Conditionals

A conditional is a sentence using 'if'.

## Zero conditional (*If you walk, it takes ten minutes*)

The zero conditional is used to describe causes and effects that are always true. We use the present simple in both halves of the sentence.

> If it rains, you get wet. (cause = rain, effect = get wet)

## First conditional (*If you walk, you'll lose weight*)

The first conditional is used for realistic possibilities. We use the present simple with the cause, and *will* with the effect.

> If I save enough money, I'll go on holiday to Croatia. (cause = save money, effect = I'll go on holiday)

You can reverse the clauses too.

> We'll make a good profit if we invest in Dubai. (cause = invest in Dubai, effect = make a good profit)

## Second conditional (*If we walked to their office, it would take hours*)

The second conditional is used for unrealistic and hypothetical situations.

> If you made Chris the sales manager, the board would never agree to his appointment. (unrealistic situation, cause = made Chris the sales manager, effect = would never agree)
> If the country had a population of 20 million, it would be a really good market. (hypothetical situation, cause = had a population of 20 million, effect = be a really good market)

Sometimes we give advice using *if I were you* …

> If I were you, I wouldn't tell them anything.

## Third conditional (*If I had walked, I would have been late*)

The third conditional is used for past possibilities.

> If I hadn't got the taxi, I would have missed my flight. (cause = hadn't got the taxi, result = would have missed flight)

It can be a difficult structure to understand.

> If Richard had known about the meeting, he would have come. (Richard didn't know, so he didn't come)

## Mixed conditional (*If I had walked, I wouldn't be here now*)

We use mixed conditionals when we want to talk about a past possibility with a present result.

> If Susannah hadn't left the company, we wouldn't be in this mess now. (past possibility = Susannah hadn't left the company, present result = we wouldn't be in this mess now)
> If you had asked yesterday, we would already know the answer. (past possibility = you had asked yesterday, present result = we would already know)

# Passives

The passive is used for various reasons. It is made with the usual verb tense of *be* + past participle.

> She was criticized by the boss yesterday. (usual tense of *be* is past simple = was, past participle = criticized)
> Rebecca will be made the new manager tomorrow. (usual tense of *be* is will = will be, past participle = made)

We may use a passive when we don't know who did an action.

> My bag has been stolen! (we don't know who stole the bag)

We may use a passive when the person who did an action is not important to us.

> My brother has been sacked from his company! (= the speaker is interested in his brother, not who sacked his brother)

We may use a passive to describe a process, such as the manufacture of a product.

> The oranges are picked in Florida. Then they are transported by road to the factory, where they are pressed by machines to make orange juice. (passive verbs = are picked, are transported, are pressed)

In a passive sentence, if we want to include who did the action, we use *by*.

> My brother has been sacked from his company by the new boss! (who did the action = the new boss)

# grammar bank

## Articles

### The indefinite article (*a, an*)

Use *a / an* to talk about something for the first time.

> I met a new client yesterday. (= first mention of the new client)
>
> There was a man waiting for you at reception. (= we have never talked about the man before)

Use *a / an* to define something.

> A cayman is a kind of crocodile. (definition of a cayman)

Use *a / an* when ordering one of something.

> I'd like an orange juice and a croissant please. (more common than **one orange juice and one croissant**)

### The definite article (*the*)

Use *the* when you talk about an object and you expect the other person to know exactly what / who you are talking about.

> I enjoyed the restaurant last night. (= everyone knows which restaurant we are talking about)
>
> Have you sent the report to the Spanish office yet? (= everyone knows which report this is)

Use *the* after mentioning something for the first time.

> There was a man waiting for you at reception. I think he was the man who came to the meeting yesterday. (first time mentioned = a man, second time, etc. = the man)

Use *the* when there is only one of something.

> Can you pass me the pen over there? (= there is only one pen which could be passed)

Many nouns use the structure *the ____ of ____*.

> the Bank of England, the Republic of Ireland, the CEO of IBM

### No article

General descriptions of uncountable nouns do not use an article.

> Sugar is grown in Cuba. (uncountable noun = sugar)

General descriptions of countable nouns do not use an article. The countable noun becomes plural.

> Computers have made our lives much, much easier. (countable noun = computers)

## Modal verbs

Modal verbs are a kind of auxiliary verb that we use to show ability, obligation, or opinion. They include *can, could, may, might, should, ought to, have to, must*, and *need to*.

> We can't hold the meeting in August because everyone will be on holiday. (can't = ability)
>
> Thomas ought to help with the production of the prototype. (ought to = the speaker's opinion)

Modal verbs are followed by the bare infinitive (i.e. the infinitive without *to*).

> You should leave at four. (should = modal, leave = bare infinitive)
>
> He must read this report before he goes to Bellinzona. (must = modal, read = bare infinitive)
>
> The illustrators might send you the pictures in PDF format. (might = modal, send = bare infinitive)

### *Have to* and *need to*

*Have to* and *need to* are exceptions.

> The letters have to be filed at head office.
>
> We need to have a discussion about this.

*Need* can also be used with *-ing*.

> The office really needs painting.

### *Have to* and *must*

In the present tense *have to* and *must* have a very similar meaning. It is more common to use *have to*.

> I must email Yukiko.
>
> I have to email Yukiko.

However, in the negative the meanings are different. *Don't have to* means 'you can choose'.

> You don't have to wear a tie to work – most people don't. (= it's your choice to wear a tie or not)

The negative of *must* means '*do not*' – forbidden.

> You mustn't take files marked 'confidential' outside the building. (= do not take the files outside the building)

### Past modals

In the past, modal verbs are followed by *have* + past participle.

> I should have got his telephone number before he left. (should = modal, have, past participle = got)
>
> He may have been in the office last weekend. (may = modal, have, been = past participle)

### Past of *could* and *was / were able to*

To talk about ability in the past use *could* or *was / were able to*. *Could* is used to mean 'general ability'.

> I could play the guitar when I was seven. (I had the general ability to play the guitar)

*Was / were able to* is used to talk about specific ability in particular occasions or events.

> It was only because I worked till three a.m. last night that I was able to deal with all the paperwork. (on this particular occasion he dealt with the paperwork)

### Past of *have to* and *must*

To talk about past obligation use *had to*.

> I had to change planes three times to fly to Patagonia. (had to = past obligation)
>
> Before we had computers, we had to write all the letters on typewriters, and it took forever! (had to = past obligation)

Use *must have* + past participle to make hypotheses about the past, when you are very certain.

> Jo must have stayed at the Bristol Hotel last night. (past modal = must, have, past participle = stayed, the speaker is certain Jo stayed at the Bristol)
>
> Wilhelm must have told them about the appointment – because only he and I know about it. (past modal = must, have, told = past participle, the speaker is certain Wilhelm told them)

# listening script

## 1.1

**Alvaro Gómez**  Hello. I'd like to speak to Susan Crawley, please.

**Susan Crawley**  Speaking.

**Alvaro Gómez**  Hello Susan. It's Alvaro Gómez from Detecsys Systems here. I'm afraid you still haven't paid for the computers we installed three months ago.

**Susan Crawley**  Ah yes, Alvaro. We seem to have lost the invoice. Would you mind sending me a duplicate?

**Alvaro Gómez**  Susan, we've already sent you two duplicate invoices and now we'd like you to pay for the computers.

**Susan Crawley**  Alvaro, I'm afraid we're having some cash-flow problems right now. Do you think you could wait until next month?

**Alvaro Gómez**  I'm under some serious pressure from my company to collect payment for this equipment, Susan. We expect you to pay before the end of June.

**Susan Crawley**  Don't worry, Alvaro. We're waiting on payment of a big project ourselves, and that's the reason for our delay.

**Alvaro Gómez**  OK Susan, we can give you another two weeks, but if we don't receive payment by then, I'm afraid we'll have to send someone round to pick up the computers.

**Susan Crawley**  That won't be necessary, Alvaro. I can assure you we'll have the money by then.

**Alvaro Gómez**  I'll take your word for it. I'll call you again in two weeks if I don't hear from you before then. Goodbye Susan.

**Susan Crawley**  OK, Alvaro.

## 1.2

1  I need you to repeat my last order for ink for the Deskjet 840C. I'm afraid you sent me black cartridges instead of colour ones and it really is quite urgent.

2  Jack, do you think I could have next Friday off, please? I've got to go to the bank to sign the mortgage for our new house.

3  I'd like a return ticket to Oxford, please.

4  Head office hasn't received the report yet, and I'd like to receive it before you leave tonight.

## 2.1

**Consultant**  So, thank you very much for all your help and cooperation during our recent visit to your company. It was a very interesting experience to see so much in such a short time. Now I'd like to go on and outline our initial proposals very briefly. First of all, we would like to propose a change to the company's name. Now we understand that it is the name of the founder of the company but we feel that the name 'Bruston Bicycles and Cycling Accessories' is not exactly a commercial name. We suggest changing to a more international name. Something that's shorter and easier to remember. Secondly, we'd like to propose that you recruit new sales staff. We know that the present sales manager is doing a great job, but she doesn't have the necessary resources. We recommend that you employ three new assistant staff – people with languages and experience in the sector. Our third proposal is to investigate the possible use of the Internet as a marketing tool for your company. We know it's not the answer to everything but we do believe that it could help to develop the company. Finally, we recommend taking serious and immediate measures to reorganize the production side of the company. There are too many long delays and you are losing clients as a result. Are there any questions at this stage before I go into detail about our proposals?

## 2.2

**Sales manager**  So, what ideas have you got then? I think we really need your help.

**Consultant**  Have you considered changing the name? It's not really commercial is it?

**Sales manager**  Yes, it's one of the many things we have discussed.

**Consultant**  Sales and Production just don't get together often enough. You've got big problems there. What about making meetings more frequent? Once a week as a minimum. They have to plan the production together!

**Sales manager**  Yes, you're right there – nobody knows what's going on really.

**Consultant**  Yes, I think you've got a big communications problem. You've got to do something about that.

**Sales manager**  Yes, I know, I know.

**Consultant**  And, well, I don't really know how to say this politely, but …

**Sales manager**  Yes? Come on! Say exactly what you think!

**Consultant**  Well, Mr Bruston's simply too old. How about getting somebody younger to do his job?

**Sales manager**  And what would we do with Mr Bruston?

**Consultant**  What if you made him president? Then you could leave the day-to-day running to a younger person.

**Sales manager**  I'll have to think about that. Anything else?

**Consultant**  You need to get more up-to-date. Have you considered using the Internet at all? And then there's the problem of design. Let's face it, some of your products look really old. What if you employed a new designer? I suggest getting someone from abroad. Someone with new ideas.

## 3.1

### 1

**Man**  I can't stand it any longer!

**Woman**  Why? What's up?

**Man**  I've just been out for lunch with Phil and I had to pay for his meal yet again.

**Woman**  Well, you could just ask him for the money.

**Man**  No, I'd rather not do that. It would be really embarrassing.

### 2

**Woman**  Why are you looking so angry?

**Man**  Michelle's smoking again and I hate it!

**Woman**  Have you told her that?

**Man**  No, I'm not sure that's such a good idea. She is the boss after all!

### 3

**Woman**  I feel really uncomfortable with Juan.

**Man**  Mmm. Me too.

**Woman**  He's always shouting and swearing, isn't he? Frankly, I've had enough of it.

**Man**  I know! Let's do the same all afternoon and see if he likes it.

**Woman**  OK. That might work, I suppose.

### 4

**Woman**  I've got a headache! Sue's been talking to her boyfriend on the phone again. You can't imagine what they were talking about!

**Man**  Why don't you turn up the radio when she's on the phone? When she asks you what you're doing, you could tell her you don't want to listen to her phone calls.

**Woman**  What a good idea! I'll do that next time he calls.

## 3.2

### 1

**Woman**  This is just so unfair!

**Man**  What is?

**Woman**  Here I am working away since eight o'clock this morning to finish this report, and John walks in at twelve expecting to leave at five to pick up his kids. There's no way we'll finish on time!

**Man**  I think you should tell your boss. It's his problem, not yours.

**Woman**  I'd rather not have to do that, actually. John would never speak to me again.

# listening script

**2**

**Jo** I wish Bill would stop taking my things. I don't mind him borrowing something, as long as he puts it back again afterwards.

**Dan** Mmm. He does the same to me, too. I know! Let's play a joke on him. Let's hide everything on his desk while he's at lunch. That way he might get the message.

**Jo** That's a good idea. Even if it doesn't work, we'll have a laugh. Shall we do it now?

**Dan** Yeah, let's.

**3**

**Ann** I don't think I can work with Ged any more.

**Al** Why's that?

**Ann** He does absolutely nothing all morning, and then disturbs me all afternoon when I'm trying to work.

**Al** You could always ask for a transfer to another department.

**Ann** I don't think that's such a good idea, actually. I really like my job, and I don't see why I should move just because of him.

**4**

**Woman** Andy is driving me absolutely crazy!

**Man** Oh dear. What's happened now?

**Woman** He just won't stop talking about his kids. Honestly, you would think nobody else in the office had any, the way he goes on.

**Man** Well, perhaps he doesn't realize he's doing it. Why don't you talk to him about it?

**Woman** Yes, that might work, I suppose. It'd be better than doing nothing, anyway.

## 4.1

**1**

**Managing director** Right, OK, well, before we start, I'd just like to say I'm very pleased with how successful our stand was at the trade fair on Friday. The stand looked pretty good – and, Jane, you did very well to get such a good location. It made such a difference.

**Jane** Yeah, I think it did.

**Managing director** Well done, Jane. And Alan – you spent most of your time looking after visitors. Well, we've been quite busy with email and phone enquiries already this morning. In fact, I can tell you that we've already taken several large orders from people who visited the stand!

**Alan** That's excellent!

**Jane** Yeah, that's really good news.

**Managing director** Great. Well done everybody!

**2**

**Jenny** Hi Tim. How are you getting along?

**Tim** Well not bad – it's quite difficult to remember everyone's name, but I'm getting there!

**Jenny** Oh, don't worry. By the way, I want to tell you how much I enjoyed your presentation yesterday. You did a great job.

**Tim** Really?

**Jenny** Yes – absolutely! In fact, everybody thought it was absolutely fantastic! We've already tried out some of your time-saving ideas in our department. It's really going to improve efficiency.

**Tim** Well, I was fairly pleased with it. Anyway, thanks for your support!

**Jenny** You're welcome!

**3**

**Boss** Ah, John, thanks for stopping by. Hope you're not too rushed?

**John** No, it's fine.

**Boss** I just wanted to mention … I've been chatting to Philippe in Paris, and they're already asking if we can send another pack of brochures through. They're extremely popular there, it seems.

**John** Oh, really? That's a surprise.

**Boss** Well … maybe, but I really liked the way you included the customer stories. Anyway, they love it – you've done very well.

**John** Well … , if you think so!

**Boss** I do! Anyway, can I ask you to give Philippe a call in Paris? He'll be in for the rest of the day.

**John** OK, and thanks!

## 4.2

**1**

**Boss** Oh, John – I just wanted to mention … That report you did was really quite good – not too long, but to the point. And on time!

**John** Oh, thanks! I'm glad you liked it!

**Boss** I'm sure head office will be really pleased.

**John** Oh good!

**2**

**Boss** Tina – good to see you.

**Tina** Oh, hello!

**Boss** By the way, congratulations on getting the new contract. We've been trying for years with that company. It's absolutely terrific!

**Tina** Oh, well, thanks very much. It took a while.

**Boss** But we got there in the end. It's really brilliant of you. Anyway, very well done.

## 5.1

**1**

**Manager** Really, Adam. This is terrible. We have customers waiting outside in the cold. There's no reason to make them wait so long. We open at nine –

it's not as difficult as all that! It was even later this morning. Just because you can't get out of bed in time. What are you going to do about it? Well?

**Adam** Yeah, but maybe I can expl–

**Manager** No 'buts'. There's no excuse. You've just got to be here on time in future. Don't let it happen again. I've no more to say.

**Adam** Well, I realize …

## 5.2

**Manager** Oh, Adam. Have you got a minute?

**Adam** Yes, of course.

**Manager** I'm afraid it's about timing again. As you are aware, we open at nine. We can't keep our customers waiting. I must insist that you arrive on time to let them in.

**Adam** Yeah, I'm sorry, um …

**Manager** Is there something making it difficult? Do you think you could get here earlier?

**Adam** Yes, of course. There are road works at the moment, so it's not as quick as before.

**Manager** Well, I'm sorry, but please do get here on time.

**Adam** Yes. I'll do my best.

## 5.3

**1**

**Woman** Thanks for making time to talk.

**Man** That's fine! How can I help?

**Woman** Well, it's just that … I'm quite busy at the moment.

**Man** I know! You've been doing some great work, really.

**Woman** Oh, good, good. The thing is, as you know, I can't really stay late at work because of the children. I have to plan my work very carefully. I'm under such a lot of pressure …

**Man** Right.

**Woman** … so I'd be grateful if we could fix times to discuss work. Just that, well, could you please try not to interrupt me when I'm working? It makes it hard to fit in my work.

**Man** Oh, right. Of course, I'd no idea. I am sorry.

**Woman** Well, do you think we could have a meeting once a week – say, Tuesdays?

**Man** Oh, OK. Maybe Wednesdays? At eleven?

**Woman** Yes, that'd be fine.

**Man** Good. Well, that's tomorrow then! OK?

**Woman** Yes, thank you.

**2**

**Sue** Could I have a word?

**James** Yes, sure.

**Sue** OK. Well. It's about the report you sent.

**James** Yes …? Um, I sent it to head office on Friday …

**Sue** Yes. Thank you. I know you haven't had much experience in this area.

**James** No, but …

**Sue** Well, maybe I can point out one or two things. Head office don't need so much information: they only need the key points, so you don't need to include so much detail. It doesn't need to be nearly as long as that.

**James** Oh, right. OK.

**Sue** Perhaps I can show you one of Mike's reports? It's a bit more target-focused. I think it would make it easier for you. Do you think you could try next time?

**James** OK. Thank you.

**Sue** Good. I'll send it through before the end of today. OK?

**James** Yes, thanks very much.

## 5.4

**Boss** Alan, have you got a minute?

**Alan** Yes, of course.

**Boss** Well, I'm afraid it's about your jeans again.

**Alan** Oh, I thought it might be.

**Boss** Well, as you know, jeans are not suitable for the office. We've talked about this before.

**Alan** Yes. We have. Sorry.

**Boss** Well, could you please try not to wear jeans again at work?

## 6.1

**Rajiv** So, Davina, how is the training going?

**Davina** So far, so good.

**Rajiv** OK. The first thing is that people don't realize that they're phoning India – they think they're calling their own country. If they find out and start to get worried, just tell them that they're not being charged at international call rates.

**Davina** Er?

**Rajiv** Is that clear?

**Davina** Yes, it's OK.

**Rajiv** All the answers are straightforward so long as you get the right information from the caller. And most of the problems are quite basic anyway. Now, one other thing: we have a lot of calls, so make sure they aren't any longer than they need to be. Be patient with the caller but keep an eye on the time. If the caller wants to chat a little, then you can be friendly, but keep it brief. Tell them you have another call waiting if you need to. Now, when this light goes on, it means you have a call. As soon as you press this, you're connected and you should greet the caller. Have you got that? Just watch me and ask any questions afterwards.

## 6.2

### 1

**Rajiv** Genius Call Centre, Rajiv speaking.

**Carl** Hello. I can't get into my documents or anything.

**Rajiv** What's the last thing that you've done, sir?

**Carl** Well it won't accept my password or my user name.

**Rajiv** Are you sure they're correct?

**Carl** Yes, when I type them, it says 'user name or password incorrect'. But they aren't incorrect! And this is a brand new computer! Listen, the password is –

**Rajiv** No, I don't need that, sir. Now, are you sure you haven't put the password in the user name box?

**Carl** What? Don't be … Ha! Now it works! Thank you very much! Goodbye.

**Rajiv** Goodbye.

**Davina** Wow, that was easy!

**Rajiv** Mmm … sometimes very easy solutions like that are the hardest to find. So, watch out for them. You handle the next call.

### 2

**Davina** Genius Call Centre, Davina speaking. Good morning.

**Zhen** Good morning. I'm calling from Dubai Airport and I'm having problems with my laptop. My wireless connection won't connect and I have some …

**Davina** Are you trying to connect to your webmail online?

**Zhen** Yes.

**Davina** What happens if you try to connect to the Internet?

**Zhen** When I connect to the Internet, it works. I can't get into my email.

**Davina** If you can't get into your email sir, there must be a problem with your email provider. I suggest you try again in thirty minutes.

**Zhen** I'll be flying back to Hong Kong by then … Oh well, thanks anyway. Goodbye.

**Davina** Goodbye, sir. Was that OK?

**Rajiv** Questions, fine. Be careful not to say 'good morning'. That could confuse them. Otherwise, good.

## 7.1

**Arthur** Hello David, how are you?

**David** OK, Arthur. Getting better but I still can't move around.

**Arthur** Well, you just take it easy. Everything's under control here.

**David** That's why I'm phoning you. There are several jobs that need doing.

**Arthur** Well, what are they?

**David** Somebody has to visit Samson Ltd. We have to discuss the pricing of the new contract. Could you get Rob to do that? He knows the company.

**Arthur** Just a second … Rob … Samson Ltd … discuss new pricing … OK, go on!

**David** I won't be able to go to Paris for the sales conference, so could you ask somebody to go in my place?

**Arthur** Yes, of course, no problem … Paris sales conference …

**David** And then there's the meeting with the national sales team. I know that's not until the end of next month but perhaps you could ask either Monica or Susan if they could look after that?

**Arthur** Won't you be back at work by then? If so, perhaps you'll be able to go yourself.

**David** I hope so!

**Arthur** Anything else?

**David** Yes, we need to have some more brochures printed – say about 5,000.

**Arthur** Yes, of course … I'll have Monica phone the printer's. We could get some business cards done at the same time.

**David** Good idea. And the last thing is the interviews for the new sales assistant. Can you get somebody from Personnel to deal with that for me? And that's everything. I'll give you a ring towards the end of the week. OK?

**Arthur** Yes, you just look after yourself and don't worry about work.

**David** Thanks Arthur. If you need anything, just phone.

**Arthur** Yes, I will. Bye!

**David** Bye!

## 7.2

**Arthur** OK everybody. Now, I've spoken to David this morning and he'll be off work until the end of the month, so we've all got some extra work to do. I'd like to help but I've got so much to do … Good, well … this visit to Samson Ltd … do you think you could handle that, Rob? You know the people there and you're familiar with the situation.

**Rob** Yes, OK. That's no trouble.

**Arthur** Thank you. And Susan, I'd like you to take care of the job interviews for the new post in Sales. Is that all right?

**Susan** Well, yes, but I might need some help.

**Arthur** Well, perhaps I could get somebody to give you a hand. Good, now I need somebody to deal with brochures for the trade fair. We need to get about 5,000 printed. Could I leave that with you, Monica? Oh, and have them do 500 business cards for each of us, too.

# listening script

**Monica** Of course, but what about the sales team meeting? Shall I look after that as well?

**Arthur** No, that's not necessary. We can leave that to David. I'm hoping he'll be back before then.

**Monica** OK.

**Arthur** Good, so that's everything, at least the most important things.

**Rob** What about the sales conference in Paris? Who are you going to get to go in David's place?

**Arthur** Oh, I'll take care of that. Oh, by the way, I'm going to be away for a couple of days after the conference. Just ...

## 7.3

**Rob** Well, that's just typical, isn't it?

**Susan** Yes, we're all very busy and now all this!

**Rob** I mean, he must know how much work we've got right now and then this Samson visit ... 'do you think you could handle that, Rob?' It's just too much!

**Susan** Yes, but ... we'll manage – we always do.

**Rob** But it's always the same with him! 'I'd like you to take care of that' ... 'Could you look after that for me, Monica?' ... 'Can I leave that with you, Susan?' ... but then he's taking a few days' holiday and going to the Paris conference!

**Susan** Yes, he didn't delegate that one! Well, let's just hope David's back soon.

**Rob** Yeah ... ah well, back to work. See you later.

**Susan** Just a moment! What about these coffee cups? Who's going to wash them up?

**Rob** Oh, could I leave that with you Susan? I'm sure you can manage.

## 8.1

**Derek** Phew! Busy night, isn't it?

**Ayse** It's like this every Friday and Saturday. You should be happy. Derek, can I speak to you for a moment, please?

**Derek** Yeah, yeah, what is it?

**Ayse** Derek, I had a phone call this afternoon from Turkey ...

**Derek** Ah yes, everything OK?

**Ayse** No. There's a big family problem at home.

**Derek** I see. Go on.

**Ayse** And I have to go back to help sort it out.

**Derek** What! Hang on, hang on – how long would you be away for?

**Ayse** I can't say – I really can't.

**Derek** Well, give me an idea.

**Ayse** I can't say – I don't know ... three weeks, maybe four ...

**Derek** Three or four weeks! When would this be?

**Ayse** As soon as possible. Tomorrow maybe ...

**Derek** Ayse, you're not serious. You can't do this to me. If you went for that long – so many weeks – you'd be leaving me in a terrible mess. You know this is the busiest month of the year.

**Ayse** Yes I know, Derek. I'll take leave without pay, so it won't cost you anything. And I'll come back as soon as I can. I don't want to lose this job, but my family needs me. And I can't say no. I have to go.

## 8.2

**Derek** Look Ayse. If you went now, I'd be without my manager for – what did you say? – a month? You must know that that's impossible.

**Ayse** Derek, I know it's inconvenient ...

**Derek** Inconvenient, Ayse! It's more than inconvenient!

**Ayse** There's a family crisis in my home. I am part of my family. If I didn't go now, what would I be? What would they think of me? They need me. Can you understand?

**Derek** You know most of the staff are new, and they don't speak much English. I don't speak Turkish. We've got three restaurants – this one's only been open for two months. I can't let you go so soon, for so long. If it were any other time of the year, it would be OK, but ...

**Ayse** I know it's a busy time of year, I do. I appreciate it from your point of view. But put yourself in my shoes – imagine if it were your family and you were in Turkey, what would you do?

**Derek** OK, OK, Ayse – this is what I suggest. Let's both sleep on it and I'll phone you tomorrow morning, and we'll talk about it, and see if we can reach some sort of compromise. Is that all right?

**Ayse** I'll be here at 9.30.

## 8.3

**Ayse** Izmir restaurant. Good morning.

**Derek** Good morning, Ayse. It's me.

**Ayse** Hello Derek.

**Derek** Right, er ... I've been doing some thinking, and I understand that it's necessary for you to be with your family for a while. On the other hand, I need someone with your experience and ability with the staff and the customers, and the accounts and the orders. So what I suggest is – if you went in four days' time that would give us time to show the ropes to someone else – a bit ...

**Ayse** What ropes?

**Derek** I mean, explain how things work, train up one of the waiters to do the cash, and then if you could promise me you'll only be away for – say – two weeks ...

**Ayse** OK, I'll stay and – what is it? – show somebody the ropes for four days, if you give me a bit more time away. Two weeks just isn't realistic. You don't know my family. Let's say I'll stay here for four days if you let me have two and a half to three weeks away, depending on flights. And if you can't accept that, well ...

**Derek** All right, Ayse, let's agree to that then. I suppose I could come in some nights. And I'll lend you the money for the flight and expenses if you like.

## 8.4

**Nimo** Hello Stavros. Actually, I'm phoning about our last invoice. You know the one I mean, it's ...

**Stavros** Yes, Nimo, of course, I'm sorry about that. We've been having some problems with late payers but I have to pay the salaries. On the other hand, our cash-flow situation ... will improve in the near future.

**Nimo** Well I'm pleased to hear that, Stavros. Of course I appreciate your situation, and I know you always pay, but this invoice is now four months ...

**Stavros** Four months! Oh, that's terrible. Is it really?

**Nimo** I'm afraid it is. So what I suggest is this – if you pay half of it this month, and the other half next month, you won't have to pay the whole amount in one go.

**Stavros** OK, let's agree to that, Nimo. That's a good compromise. And please accept my apologies. You know this is not typical ...

## 9.1

### 1

**Rick** So, when will the new office be ready, Kate?

**Kate** Hopefully by the summer. The contractors have assured me they'll have finished painting by the end of June. So the first thing we need to think about is when we should move.

**Rick** Surely the best time will be in August. The office will have closed for the summer by then, so we'll have the whole month to organize everything.

**Kate** I agree. So something else we have to do is get in touch with a moving company. Any ideas?

**Rick** I'll take care of that, Kate. I know a couple of companies so I'll call them and ask for a quote. Who's going to be responsible for the packing?

**Kate** I guess we can ask the moving company to do that. What do you think?

**2**

**Bob**  Well, good morning, everyone. We're here to talk about the launch of our new line of sun creams. Right now there's nothing on the market aimed specifically at teenagers, so I think this could do well.

**Tony**  Have we decided on a name yet, Bob?

**Bob**  No name yet, but Design have promised me they'll have thought of something by the end of the week. What we need to do now is get the advertising campaign organized.

**Ana**  Which agency are we going to use, Bob?

**Bob**  I think the best way to go about it is to ask several agencies for samples. That way we'll get a fresh new look.

**Tony**  When's the launch date?

**Bob**  The ads need to appear to coincide with the start of the good weather, so early May would be good.

## 9.2

**Woman**  So, how should we go about this presentation, then?

**Man**  I think the first thing we need to think about is where we're going to do it.

**Woman**  I'd really like them to come to us. That way they'll have seen how well equipped we are before they make a decision on the contract.

**Man**  Who's going to give the presentation, anyway?

**Woman**  Well, I don't mind giving it as long as you and your team take care of the visuals and the figures.

**Man**  So what we need to decide next is what to include in the presentation. Do they want to know about our company in general, or do they just want to see what we can do?

## 10.1

**General director**  Heather, could you give me an update on the Italcafé pitch, please?

**Account manager**  Well, it's going quite well, actually. We've already met the managing director, and he's told us how he sees his company. We've also spoken to him about our ideas, and so far he's agreed with everything we've suggested.

**General director**  How are you getting on with the market research?

**Account manager**  We've just got the results back and we're analysing them right now. All we're waiting for now is the creative work.

**General director**  How's that going?

**Account manager**  Well, the creative team should have shown me their ideas for the advertising campaign this morning, but they haven't met the date again, so we've put our meeting back to tomorrow.

**General director**  Have you decided which media you're going to use yet?

**Account manager**  Yes, I think it's going to be basically radio and television. Up to now, we've only managed to contact two of the television companies. We're in the process of speaking to radio stations and they seem quite interested.

**General director**  So, when is the presentation going to be?

**Account manager**  We've already made a provisional date for next Friday. Will you be able to make it?

**General director**  Yes, I'll be there. Keep me posted.

## 10.2

**Woman**  How are you getting on with the marketing campaign?

**Man**  Well, it's not going very well, actually. I haven't really met the target we agreed on.

**Woman**  Oh dear. What's gone wrong?

**Man**  Well, I've ordered some new leaflets, but they haven't arrived yet, so I can't send them out.

**Woman**  What about the email promotion? How's that going?

**Man**  I've sent about twenty emails so far, but up to now I haven't had any replies.

**Woman**  Have you decided how to go about the telephone campaign?

**Man**  Yes, I'm in the process of drawing up a list of companies to call. I think it'll be ready by tomorrow afternoon.

**Woman**  OK. Show me the list when you've finished and I'll see if I can add any more.

## 11.1

**Mike**  So let's go through the figures for Home Sales this year. Tony?

**Tony**  Thanks, Mike. Well, it's been a strange year so far. As you can see from the chart, sales were very good, excellent in fact, at the beginning of the year. They went up by 12.6% and we sold over 6,500 units between January and March, but then the next quarter was quite slow with an increase of only a disappointing 5.4%. This last third quarter has been a bit better and sales are up by 9.2%. However, the forecast for sales in the final quarter is just 7,050 units, an increase of only 4.7%, which means that we should end the year with an overall increase of under 8%. Short of our target, I'm afraid.

**Mike**  Well, we'll have to discuss that later on this morning but let's hear about Export Sales now. Susan …

## 11.2

**Mike**  Well, we'll have to discuss that later on this morning but let's hear about Export Sales now. Susan?

**Susan**  Well, I'm very pleased to say that the Export Market is doing really well. As you know, the first two quarters this year were excellent with increases of 8.8% and a fantastic 15.4% over the same periods for last year. The sales figures for the last quarter have just come in and I'm delighted to tell you that we have been able to sell over 9,000 units for the first time in the history of the department, a great result which represents an increase of 11.4%. The forecast for the final quarter is also very promising. We expect an increase in sales of 13.5% with unit sales of 7,500, and that's a conservative estimate for the next three months which, if everything goes well, will mean an annual increase of 12.35% for this year, well over our initial target of 7.5%. Obviously, I'm really happy about the way the department has been working this year. We have done really well in eastern Europe and the new Madrid office has increased its sales by over 20% since January, which is a fantastic performance. Now I'd like to mention a few people who …

## 12.1

**1**

A  We missed you at the meeting yesterday.

B  I was going to call but, you know I was having lunch with a client. We had a drink. We had to wait ages for service, and, one thing led to another. You know what it's like.

**2**

C  Morning!

D  Afternoon.

C  It's only eleven.

D  But your normal working hours are ten to six. You're always arriving late! What's the excuse this time?

C  You're never going to believe it. It's never happened before, but my bus broke down on the way in. I had to walk.

**3**

F  Right, I'm going home.

E  Ah, I'm looking for you! Could I have a word? Were you responsible for the new brochure?

# listening script

**F** Er... Yes.

**E** And you were responsible for the spell check?

**F** On the computer. It seemed fine.

**E** Could you explain then why there are at least three spelling mistakes on the cover? And we've printed 5,000 copies.

**F** Right. Er, yes, I checked the content but Sue was supposed to do the cover, and you know, she was sick. I don't know what could have happened.

**E** This could conceivably cost the company £1,000.

## 12.2

### 1

**Paula** I got the cheque OK, Oliver, but there's no signature.

**Oliver** Oh no! When I wrote the cheque, I was rushing to catch the last post and, one thing led to another. I'll send you another as soon as possible. I am extremely sorry about this, believe me.

### 2

**Franco** So we've got a problem. The invoice has arrived and the units are right but the currency is wrong. It's written in dollars, but I thought it would be in euros.

**Ray** Oh no! I know what's happened. We were writing the American orders at the same time as we were processing the Italian invoices. If you just send us the payment, with that price in euros, it's fine.

**Franco** Great. We'll do that.

## 13.1

**Man** Hello, you're late! Everything OK?

**Woman** Sorry, I had to leave the car at the garage and get the bus.

**Man** The garage! What's wrong this time?

**Woman** It wouldn't start. They say there's something wrong with the starter motor.

**Man** And last week it was the battery; the month before, the suspension. This car's costing us a fortune!

**Woman** Yes, I know. Listen, darling. Why don't we get a new one?

**Man** A new one! Do you think we can afford it?

**Woman** That's not the question, is it? We're spending too much on repairs. We simply have to get rid of it and get a new one.

**Man** But if we get a new one, what about the holiday in Miami? We can't afford to go to Miami and buy a new car at the same time, can we?

**Woman** No, obviously, if we buy a new one, we won't be able to go to Miami. But the way I see it we've got no choice but to get a new car. Miami will have to wait.

**Man** OK, we can talk about it after dinner.

**Woman** Yes, er ... do you need your car tomorrow?

## 13.2

**Ali** Listen Tom – can I have a word with you?

**Tom** Yes, of course, Ali. What's up?

**Ali** Well, I've just been speaking to Tony Davies from JPC about their new plant in China.

**Tom** Ah yes? When are they planning to open?

**Ali** At the end of next year, but I think we may have a problem there.

**Tom** Really? What's the problem?

**Ali** Well, they want to know if we have thought about China as well.

**Tom** China? In what way?

**Ali** Well, reading between the lines, I think that if we don't have a factory there in a couple of years, they'll look for another supplier, someone local. It's the transport costs to China – they are simply too high.

**Tom** Well China's a long way away, isn't it?

**Ali** Yes, but unless we can supply them from within China, I think we'll lose them.

**Tom** Oh I'm sure we can arrange something – better terms ...

**Ali** No, Tom. I think they've made a decision about this. I think we'll simply have to set up a small plant in China near their factory. We can't afford to lose them as clients. And JPC is not the only client who's going to China!

**Tom** But opening in China will cost us a small fortune!

**Ali** Yes I know. But we simply must do it. Otherwise we're in trouble. I told him we'd study the question seriously. But I don't think we have much choice but to open up there, and pretty quickly!

**Tom** Have you spoken to the others about this?

**Ali** No, just you. I've only just got back from JPC.

**Tom** Well, we'd better have a meeting as soon as possible.

## 14.1

### 1

**Adam** Webshakers. Good afternoon. Adam speaking.

**Mansoor** Oh, hello, Adam. This is Mansoor here from Frozen Foods Fast.

**Adam** Ah, Mansoor, how are things? I tried to return your call this morning but I couldn't get hold of you.

**Mansoor** Oh, sorry about that. You must have called during our monthly update meeting.

**Adam** So this is concerning the website?

**Mansoor** Yeah, it is. There are a couple of things I'd like to discuss.

**Adam** Right. OK. So how can we help?

**Mansoor** Well, my main concern is the time it's taking for your people to make changes to the material we sent you.

**Adam** Oh right. I didn't know about this. It could have been because of some problems we've had in moving our systems over to the new servers. In any case, I can look into this and get back to you.

**Mansoor** Great. We now also have a number of new sections we'd like to add, and they're quite complicated, so ... I was wondering ... could I suggest we meet sometime next week to talk them through?

**Adam** Yes, that'd be fine.

### 2

**Mansoor** Well, Adam. It's good of you to come over. Thanks.

**Adam** My pleasure. And I've had a look into what's been going on.

**Mansoor** Right. Good. Well, I realize now perhaps we shouldn't have turned down your offer of two years ago – you remember? – about controlling our own online ordering service ...

**Adam** Ah, yes. I remember. It must have been too expensive at the time. Well, we could offer you an updated version of the content management toolbox now.

**Mansoor** Well, actually... I'm not sure. How long would it take to install the management toolbox? The thing is, time's our priority at the moment.

**Adam** OK. Well, we could do it within about two months – that'd run at price band B, up from price band D, which is what your present site runs at.

**Mansoor** Mm ... that's still a little expensive ... and two months is really too long. The main thing is we need to be able to edit the web pages fast.

**Adam** OK. Well, listen, give me a couple of days.

**Mansoor** OK. When can you get back to me?

**Adam** By the end of the week? What would be the best means of contacting you?

**Mansoor** I prefer email because I'll be away from my desk a lot this week ....

### 3

**Adam** Mansoor? Adam here. Did you get the draft proposal? I couriered it to you last night.

**Mansoor** Oh, sorry about that. You

**Mansoor** No, I haven't seen it, but it might have arrived already. I'll check with reception.

**Adam** Anyway, I've had another look at what we could do for you. And, well, we can probably install the toolbox the end of next month, I'd say.

**Mansoor** Well, that sounds much more reasonable. Oh, and the price?

**Adam** Well, I think we could do it at the top end of price band C, but it may not have all the functionality you might want.

**Mansoor** Well, that sounds fine. What would we be missing out on?

## 15.1

**David** Good morning, everybody! I have an excellent piece of news for you all! It gives me great pleasure to announce that the prototype of the new A471 has passed all the tests with far fewer problems than we expected, and we are now ready to put it into production. I have samples of the new model here for you to have a look at, and Helen, our technical manager, is here to tell you about the main improvements. But first, I'd like to thank all the design team for their excellent work. I'm absolutely certain that the new model will be a bestseller within a very short time. Now Helen?

## 15.2

**Helen** Thank you, David. I would like to highlight a few of the most significant improvements of the new model. The A471 is much lighter than the old model – it's only 140 grams in fact, just a little heavier than a bar of chocolate – and it's a lot slimmer than before, measuring only ten by four by two centimetres, which is slightly smaller than a packet of aspirin. The best news however, is the increased memory, which is now an enormous five gigabytes – that's five times bigger than the old model! And I'm delighted to tell you all that the use of new materials means a big reduction in production costs. The A471 will be considerably cheaper to manufacture – around 25% less in fact. This, of course, should make the final sale price of the A471 about $15 cheaper than the A47, which I'm sure will be great news for all our clients. If we look at the technical characteristics ...

## 15.3

**Chris** Chris Harris.
**Peter** Hello Chris. This is Peter from AP.
**Chris** Hello Peter.
**Peter** I'm phoning because I think I've got some really good news for you.

**Chris** Ah yes?
**Peter** Yes, we have a new improved model of the A47. The A471. You'll be pleased to hear that it's much lighter and smaller, and it comes with a far bigger memory.
**Chris** That sounds very interesting. The A47 is OK but we need a lot more memory power.
**Peter** Yes, but that's not the best news, Chris! I'm sure you'll be delighted to know that we can offer you a much better price!
**Chris** Now, that is good news!
**Peter** Yes, we think it'll be around 10% cheaper for you.
**Chris** 10%!
**Peter** Yes, I told you I had good news. Listen, could I visit you this week and show you some samples?
**Chris** Yes of course, I'll be free on Friday morning. At around 11.00?
**Peter** I'd prefer a bit earlier. Say 10.00?
**Chris** OK, 10.00 it is. See you on Friday! Bye, and thanks for phoning!
**Peter** My pleasure! Bye!

## 16.1

**Natalia** Wow, I'm exhausted.
**Jake** So am I. But I really enjoyed it.
**Natalia** We seemed to have many more visitors than last year.
**Matt** Yes. Jake, could you check up on specific numbers before next week?
**Jake** Sure. I would have done it this morning if I hadn't had a last minute phone call.
**Matt** OK. Did every visitor leave their name and contact details?
**Jake** Most of them. But if I'd been more insistent, I could have asked a lot more people to sign up. Still, it made a huge difference to have the artist signing sessions after the performances. Those drew big crowds, and really helped sales. Next time let's get really big posters to promote them.
**Matt** One thing we must rethink is the papering.
**Natalia** You mean the leaflets?
**Matt** Yes. We should think it through better in terms of quantity and distribution. The boys who did that worked very hard, but I think a lot of leaflets were left around as rubbish.
**Jake** Yes. If we'd been more specific about where to distribute them in the first place, it wouldn't have happened.
**Natalia** And we didn't have enough for the whole week. But the balloons were good.
**Matt** Yes, they were a great idea, Natalia. Thanks! Anyway, I'd better be going. I'll see you both tomorrow. And let's finalize all the data for the evaluation meeting next week. OK?

**Natalia** OK. See you.

## 16.2

**Matt** OK, then. Let's see what we've got. First, perhaps we could go through sales data, stand activities, and a breakdown of visitors to the stand. And then let's take a look at the website hits, promotional materials, and press coverage. OK?
**Jake** Fine. Shall I start with sales?
**Matt** Yes, go ahead.
**Jake** Well, sales of Asian and Middle Eastern music easily topped the rest. We could have doubled our sales, I think.
**Matt** So next year double orders for that range?
**Jake** Uh huh. Erm ... Sadly we ran out of copies of the Japanese drummers, but I've taken orders on those. Here's a printout of sales by region. And on the next page you've got sales by label.
**Matt** Thanks. Uh-huh. I'm surprised that we didn't take any advance orders for next month's new releases.
**Jake** But I think we need to make sure that our stock on the stand matches the festival's line-up of artists much better. We had no Portuguese music, and that Fado singer on the last night was fantastic.
**Natalia** Yes, she was.
**Jake** The less familiar music CDs and DVDs didn't sell so well.
**Natalia** Well, perhaps we should have had facilities to let people hear CD tracks with headphones before buying. If we'd had more listening posts, we would have sold much more this time.
**Matt** OK. I'll make a note of it for next time.
**Natalia** The loop video clips worked well, and definitely promoted DVD sales.
**Jake** Definitely. People were crowding round. We could have set up more screens for them to watch it – let's do that next time.
**Matt** Indeed. Anyway, Jake. Tell us about visitor numbers.
**Jake** OK. Well, I've got a breakdown by age, as well as by nationality, of all those who visited the stand, and who filled out a mailing-list form. And for purposes of comparison, these charts show the last two years' results too. You'll see that visitor numbers are up 20%.
**Matt** OK. So this implies that ...

## 17.1

**Robin** OK, guys ... Let's start with the issue of meetings, and then deal with the rest of the agenda. Mike – could you fill me in on this?

# listening script

**Mike**  Yeah, sure. Well, you know, we have all these meetings to attend – and Jeff never gets here on time – and at the end of the day, after hours on the road, we'd just like to get home, you know.

**Robin**  Well, I do realize you're doing a lot of mileage. I'd be very happy to try and make things easier for you.

**Jim**  Yeah, but it's the meetings! The meetings take up so much time.

**Robin**  OK, but what alternatives are there? I'd be happy to discuss it. What thoughts have you got?

**Mike**  Well, a simple option is … What if we cut the number of meetings?

**Robin**  OK. Well, maybe … Any other ideas?

**Tom**  Well, I'd rather go straight home at the end of the day, as an alternative to coming here to write up sales reports. I mean, that's my biggest problem, that I have to come into the office every evening to write the reports. Instead, I could send the sales data, which I can do in the evening, to you on email next morning.

**Robin**  Uh-huh. Would you all be able to email reports through regularly?

**Jim**  Sure. That'd be fine …

**Mike**  Yeah, I should think so.

**Robin**  Right, OK. Well, let's try some of these ideas. As for meetings, well, perhaps we could meet here just once a month, or maybe every two weeks to start with. How does that sound?

**Mike**  Much better.

**Robin**  Good. Well I'll put this to the management team, and then get back to you.

## 17.2

**Chair**  OK, then. Let's move on to the next point on the agenda. Robin – this is yours, I think?

**Robin**  Er yes, that's right. Well as you can see, it's about flexible working hours, which I touched on last week.

**Anne**  You mean you want your staff to work a sixty-hour week, then?

**Robin**  No, no! Let me put it this way. There have been complaints about the number of hours that they're on the road for. So I've got a couple of ideas I'd like to suggest.

**Chair**  Right …

**Robin**  Well, one option would be for them to work partly from home, as the …

**Marcus**  Oh, that'll never work.

**Chair**  Robin, if you could just continue …

**Robin**  Thank you. Well, my team of sales reps cover hundreds of miles each week and spend nearly all day on the road, which is all very tiring. They're a good, hard-working team, but they're getting more unhappy each week, which is why I'd like to reorganize how we work. Additionally, it's an extra challenge to come back each day to write up the results of the day's work, as well as attend weekly meetings. I'd like to suggest they do some of their work from home, which I know has proved successful in other companies, and I think that will result in a much happier and more productive team.

**Marcus**  But can you really trust them to work if you can't see them?

**Robin**  Oh yes. Completely. What I'd like to offer them is greater flexibility, a weekly written reporting system, and instead of one meeting a week, we should have just one meeting a month, which will really help take the pressure off.

**Anne**  That's quite a change.

**Robin**  Well, obviously I need your support too, because you monitor individual projects as well.

**Anne**  I see. But they'll need access to the system from home, right?

**Robin**  Yes, that's right. Could you look into that for me?

**Anne**  OK. Well, I can certainly give it some thought.

**Marcus**  But what about all that space they are using? Do you want to keep that too?

**Robin**  No, no. I mean, if I could make a suggestion? The office where we work now can be used by your people in Finance. We'll only need two computer access points.

**Chair**  Well, that'd be a benefit …

## 18.1

**Malcolm**  Now, I think that's the financial situation sorted out. Now, Magda, I think you wanted to say something.

**Magda**  Thanks, Malcolm. I've been doing some thinking, and it's my opinion that, if we want to stay profitable, we should seriously consider diversifying. We make aluminium for construction and for vehicles, but there's one huge area we don't do, and that's packaging.

**Steve**  For the food industry?

**Magda**  Yes, aluminium dishes for takeaway food, aluminium foil for wrapping. There's a massive demand for it. It's a growing market, and it's growing without us.

**Steve**  It's a totally different process, Magda.

**Magda**  True. But we can't just take it easy. We have to be looking for new opportunities to grow.

**Steve**  With all due respect, Magda, it's not as simple as that. You're talking about a whole new line of business.

**Magda**  But the thing is, a company either evolves and develops, or it stagnates.

**Steve**  By and large I agree, but that doesn't mean you should risk everything on a completely new product line, new process, new technology, new space – it'd mean setting up a whole new department …

**Malcolm**  You've got a point, Steve, but on the other hand, maybe we shouldn't dismiss this idea so quickly. Who knows, Magda could be right, but the main problem for me is that we don't know the packaging sector, and it already has very established suppliers.

**Magda**  That goes without saying. But now – while we're not doing badly – is exactly when we have to diversify.

**Malcolm**  Steve?

**Steve**  Sorry, Magda, I can't agree with that. Why do we have to diversify? We're consolidating our market nicely at the moment. We're making a nice profit again. We'd have to borrow a huge amount of money without any guarantee of success.

**Malcolm**  I know what you mean, Steve. I mean, I'm not convinced yet, but I think we should have a good look at this idea before we make a decision. So, Magda, put together a business plan, and if you can come up with some conclusive reasons why we should branch out into packaging, we'll listen with an open mind, OK? Steve?

**Steve**  That's OK by me.

## 19.1

**Carl**  So, Lina … what do you think?

**Lina**  I quite like them, but I'm not really sure how many we would sell here. You see, people here aren't used to baking their own bread, and a lot will depend on the price.

**Carl**  Believe me, once you've started, people would tell their friends and family. Word of mouth, you know. You see, happy customers tend to buy another breadmaker, not for themselves but for presents.

**Lina**  Mmm … maybe. Now Carl, would there be any flexibility on those wholesale prices?

**Carl**  What do you mean?

**Lina**  You see, to be honest, I'm not sure this idea would work here. It would be a bit of a risk for us to have a lot of expensive stock. We might have stock that we can't sell! It all depends on whether we can find a good price.

**Carl** These prices are already very competitive.

**Lina** Well … I was thinking … For the KR 250, would you be able to give us 10% off the trade price?

**Carl** I can't say at this stage. If you took about 150 …

**Lina** OK, then I think we could do that. Yep, 10% off.

**Carl** And the KR 300? You'll find it very easy to sell, believe me.

**Lina** I think we'll take fifty KR 300s, at €85.50.

**Carl** Er, €85.50. Fine. Are you sure you only want fifty?

**Lina** For the time being, yes.

**Carl** The 350 at €110?

**Lina** I'm not sure whether we want to order that model yet or not. I can't order that model now. We might stock them in the future. It depends on the sales of the 250 and the 300. Oh, excuse me, Carl.

## 19.2

**Tony** So … Markus … I think there are still one or two things to sort out. How would you feel about working on Saturdays?

**Markus** Would that be necessary?

**Tony** At this stage, yes, but after the first six months, it'd probably be one Saturday in three.

**Markus** And would I get time off during the week to compensate?

**Tony** You would, or you'd get three days off at a time sometimes.

**Markus** I see. And you mentioned something about relocation?

**Tony** Yes, would you be prepared to relocate to another continent for up to two years?

**Markus** Oh! That's a long time. I mean, maybe. It really depends on whether my partner is ready to do that, and on my daughter.

**Tony** Well, we might be able to arrange a package that included schooling for your daughter at an international school wherever you were posted.

**Markus** Maybe that's a good option. But I'd like to be able to get home sometimes to see my family and friends.

**Tony** That's a bit more difficult. But of course you would have all your statutory holidays.

**Markus** Would the company help pay for flights back here?

**Tony** Well, yes. But a lot depends on whether the company keeps the present travel budget. I'm not sure we'd pay for your partner, but …

## 20.1

### Meeting 1

**Chair** Right, listen everybody, listen. Can you listen, please? Right then, what about your meetings – how did they go? Was everything OK?

**Voice 1** No it wasn't.

**Voice 2** Yes, all right, I suppose.

**Chair** Yes? Or did you have any problems?

**Voice 3** There's too many people off sick.

**Chair** What was that? Sorry, I can't hear you. Please be quiet, I can't hear. What? You think there are too many people going off sick?

**Voice 1** Load of rubbish!

**Chair** What? You mean you don't, Charlie? What do you mean you don't have a problem? Look, please be quiet, I can't hear.

### Meeting 2

**Chair** Right then, I think we should start. Now, as you all know, we're here to discuss the main issues arising from the last departmental meetings. As you can see, there are six items on today's agenda. We only have this room until 3 o'clock, so let's try to stick to the agenda. Brad, could you start by telling us about the problems we've had with unauthorized access to our intranet, and what you're thinking of doing to prevent this happening.

## 20.2

**Chair** Right then, I think we should start. Now, as you all know, we're here to discuss the main issues arising from the last departmental meetings. As you can see, there are six items on today's agenda. We only have this room until 3 o'clock, so let's try to stick to the agenda. Brad, could you start by telling us about the problems we've had with unauthorized access to our intranet, and what you're thinking of doing to prevent this happening?

…

**Martin** Isn't it obvious what the problem is? We need to ask staff to bring sick notes every time they're absent, it's simple! That will make people think twice before calling in sick.

**Susan** Actually, I think there's more to it than that. I think we need to discuss this in more detail.

…

**Susan** Paul, what do you think of Keith's proposal to outsource the cleaning staff?

**Paul** Well, we certainly can't afford to keep on the current number of staff, but I'd advise against outsourcing the cleaning completely. Maybe we could consider employing a small number of full-time cleaners, and employing the remainder through an agency.

…

**Martin** Can I just ask Paul if he remembered to ask his department to stop taking their holidays all at the same time?

**Paul** Well, I tried telling them that it was …

**Chair** Actually, I think we should move on to the next point now. Time is running short and we still have two more items to discuss.

…

**Chair** Does anyone have anything to add to that before we finish?

**Paul** I don't think so.

**Susan** No, I think that's about everything.

**Chair** OK, let's go over what we've agreed.

## 21.1

**Chair** So, let's move on to Luke's proposal for a team-building weekend. Can we hear your views on this idea, Harry?

**Harry** Frankly, I don't think it would work at all!

**Chair** Luke?

**Luke** Why not? I'm sure you must see that we have a communication problem between our different departments.

**Harry** Yes – to be fair, we don't cooperate with each other as well as we could.

**Luke** Well, in my opinion the reason for this lack of communication is, to be frank, that the heads of department just don't know each other well enough.

**Harry** That's a load of rubbish! We've been working together for years.

**Luke** Yes, but I firmly believe that the company would be far more efficient if we learnt to work together properly.

**Harry** Look, I'm sorry Luke, but I spend enough time in the office already …

**Luke** I'm glad you've brought up the question of time, Harry. That's one of my main reasons for proposing this weekend in the first place. I'm quite sure we all have similar problems with organization in our own departments, but I honestly think we waste a lot of time dealing with these problems individually instead of learning from each other's experiences.

**Harry** Yes, but realistically, Luke, have you thought of the cost …

**Luke** But don't you see this would be an investment for the company? Just think, if we all worked together more effectively, then we would be saving the company both time and money.

**Chair** I think you've got a point there, Luke.

## 21.2

**Woman** What do you think of our idea for the anniversary party then, David?

# listening script

**Man**  You mean the balloon trip?

**Woman**  Yes, and the dinner when we land.

**Man**  I think it's a ridiculous idea, to be honest.

**Woman**  Oh, go on David. I really think it'll be a lot of fun.

**Man**  Personally I think it's irresponsible. If anything goes wrong, we could be killed.

**Woman**  Well, I suppose it could be a bit dangerous, but in my opinion it's something different. There aren't many people who've been up in a hot air balloon before!

**Man**  And what happens if we get lost in the balloons? We'll never arrive for the dinner.

**Woman**  But don't you see that's part of the excitement? There'll be prizes for the first people to arrive, and there'll be plenty of time to have a drink and wait for the latecomers. You've nothing to worry about. Seriously, the balloons will be piloted by professionals.

**Man**  And what about the cost? Obviously it's not going to be cheap.

**Woman**  Oh come on. It's not every day the company celebrates its 25th anniversary. As far as I'm concerned, this is just what we need to motivate our staff to do well. And just think of all the advertising we can do on the side of the balloons. We'll be in all the newspapers, you know.

## 22.1

**Tony**  OK! OK! Listen everybody! Listen! Welcome to PJK Ltd. Thanks for coming! My name's Tony and I work in PR here at PJK. Can you all hear me? Yes? Good! Today we're going to do three things. One – the factory tour – two – a look at our products – three – lunch! … Be quiet please! Sorry? What did you say?

**Voice**  I said 'could you repeat the three things?'

**Tony**  Oh you weren't listening then? I said that the three things were … the tour … the products … then lunch. Got that? If there's anything else you don't understand, just ask. OK? Right! Come on! We've got a lot to do before we can have lunch. We can't waste time! Follow me! Hurry up!

## 22.2

**Alvaro**  Excuse me! Excuse me! Could I have your attention please? First of all, I'd like to thank you for coming today. I hope you enjoy your visit. I'd like to introduce myself. My name's Alvaro Garcia and I work in the Public Relations department of Marques de Laguardia. Can everyone hear me at the back or should I speak up? The programme that we have prepared for you today has three parts: firstly, we'll be visiting the winery where we make the wine, secondly, we'll go on to see where we store the wine in bottles and in casks, and, finally, we'll be having lunch on the terrace. I am only too happy to answer any questions you may have but before we begin the tour, if I could have your attention please, I'd like to tell you a little about what we do here. I'll try to be as brief as possible. The different wines we make have the Rioja appellation of origin or D.O. as we call it. More than 70% of the wine we produce is for export. The installations that you will see today are only five years old and are probably the most modern in Spain. The wine is stored in special tanks for the fermentation process. The small tanks you can see contain 25,000 litres of wine but the biggest tanks have a capacity for half a million litres. As you probably know, the grapes we use are grown in the well-known Rioja region of Spain. When the fermentation process is finished, the wine is stored in oak barrels or casks, as we call them. The casks we use are made from American or French oak and contain 225 litres each. It might be a little cold in the storage room where we keep the casks because the temperature has to be 16°C to ensure that the …

…

**Alvaro**  Now, if you'd like to come this way. We have to go fairly quickly.

**Voice**  Excuse me, but how long does the Gran Reserva process take?

**Alvaro**  How long does the process take? To be a Gran Reserva wine we are speaking about five years and the wine must be in an oak cask for at least three of those years. Does that answer your question? Good! Well, here we are at the restaurant area – I have to leave now, but I hope you have enjoyed your visit and I wish you all a safe and pleasant journey home. Goodbye!

## 23.1

Good afternoon everyone, and, um, thanks for coming along. I'd like to talk to you briefly today about language training options. As you know, English is to be the language of our company, and so, as a result, we'll need to work to bring everyone's English up to the required level. In spite of the size of this task, I'm confident that we can achieve this, and, what's more, that we can do it within twelve months.

…

So, I'll suggest a number of alternatives. I have identified three possibilities, which I'll talk about in detail in a moment. Firstly, I'll describe the pros and cons of continuing with the language classes as they are now. I'll then outline a scheme for sending key members of staff to attend short courses in the UK. Thirdly, we could invite a consultant in to give the company 'a language audit'. In addition, I'll summarize the company's spending on language training – specifically on English language training – over the last few years, together with the budget for coming years. Right, so, I'll run through them one by one, and outline the benefits of each. Oh, and, um, if you have any questions, perhaps you could keep them to the end. Thank you.

## 23.2

So, I'd like to move on now to talk about the final stage of the procedure. In this stage, we compare the English level of each employee to the language requirements of their post. This process is based on data we have collected, in particular on the information gathered during interviews. In most cases, this will allow staff to be placed in the most appropriate level of language class. However, as I said before, it means that some people will probably not need to continue with their language classes.

Right. OK then. Let me just remind you of the main points I've made. First, we interview all members of staff, as well as talking to each manager about the team under them. Then we carry out the language testing, and analyse the language requirements of each post. Finally, we put this information together to make recommendations about the training needs of each employee.

Well, that's all I have to say at the moment.

Thank you for your attention.

## 24.1

**Otto**  So the point is that, although your textile plant here in Barcelona produces excellent goods, they are simply no longer competitive on an international market. We've had to take the decision to rationalize our production facilities. This means that we're going to close down our plant here twelve weeks from now. All textile production will be transferred to a new factory in China. Our costs will be much lower there and the quality is comparable. Obviously, we'll keep a small office here, but we'll only need about six or seven people instead of the fifty-six who are currently employed. This is a sad moment for all of us, but times change, as you know, and I'm sure for those people who take the long-term view, this solution will be for the best.

## 24.2

**Otto**   So the point is that, although your textile plant here in Barcelona produces excellent goods, they are simply no longer competitive on an international market. We've had …

**Luisa**   Excuse me, may I interrupt?

**Otto**   Ah, yes. Go ahead.

**Luisa**   Have you considered investing in more modern machinery here?

**Otto**   That's a good point, Luisa, but it's not simply a question of machinery. Now, as I was saying, we've had to take the decision to rationalize our production facilities. This …

**Ricardo**   Otto, sorry, when you say 'rationalize', what exactly do you mean?

**Otto**   Well, Ricardo, I'm coming to that now. This means that we're going to close down our plant here twelve weeks from now …

**Luisa**   What?

**Ricardo**   Just a moment, Otto. Did you say we're going to be closed down?

**Otto**   That's right. All textile production will be transferred to a new factory in China. Our costs will be much lower there and the quality is comparable. Obviously, we'll …

**Luisa**   Excuse me, Otto, can I say something here? Are you so sure about the quality?

**Otto**   Let me emphasize that it's a question of quality and cost. Obviously, we'll …

**Ricardo**   Sorry, Otto, don't you think that twelve weeks is rather short notice? I'm sure …

**Otto**   May I just finish? Obviously, we'll keep a small office here, but we'll only need six or seven people instead of the fifty-six who are currently employed.

**Ricardo**   I'm sure you know that we've already begun production of the winter collection, and we have orders for the next thirteen months.

**Otto**   I see what you mean, Ricardo. We can find ways of fulfilling our clients' orders by means of the new factory in China. This is a sad moment for all of us, but times change, as you know, and I'm sure your experience and ability, Luisa, and yours, Ricardo, will be extremely valuable for the next

phase in the company's life. Can we count on you?

## 25.1

**Fernando López**   Excuse me. Do you mind if I sit here?

**Sofia Platini**   No. Please, go ahead.

**Fernando López**   Thanks. I'm Fernando López from the Madrid office.

**Sofia Platini**   Nice to meet you. I'm Sofia Platini from Milan.

**Fernando López**   Pleased to meet you, Sofia. Is this your first trip to London?

**Sofia Platini**   No, it's the second time I've been here, actually. I was here last year, too. Actually, I don't travel abroad very much as I work in the IT department. So I'm just enjoying being out and about.

**Fernando López**   So you keep the computer system working.

**Sofia Platini**   I look after the software, actually. I make sure everybody has what they need to do their job. What do you do, Fernando?

**Fernando López**   I'm in charge of Human Resources, so I spend most of my time in the office. It's nice to have this chance to get away! How was your flight, Sofia?

**Sofia Platini**   Fine, no problems. How about you?

**Fernando López**   Actually I nearly missed the flight because I left work late. We're very busy at the moment because we're interviewing for two new posts in Administration.

**Sofia Platini**   It's not a good time for me either because we're installing a brand new program in all the computers, and it's taking longer than we thought.

## 25.2

**Sam Isaakson**   Hello. My name's Sam Isaakson. I'm from Sweden.

**Chris Richter**   Nice to meet you, Sam. I'm Chris Richter from Germany.

**Sam Isaakson**   Pleased to meet you, Chris. Did you have a good trip?

**Chris Richter**   Not too bad. And you?

**Sam Isaakson**   Yes, apart from a short delay in the airport. Is this your first trip to New York?

**Chris Richter**   No, I've been here twice before on holiday. I'm staying in the same hotel as on my last holiday, actually. How about you?

**Sam Isaakson**   No, it's my first time. So … what do you do in Germany, Chris?

**Chris Richter**   I work for the managing director, Jens Fischer.

**Sam Isaakson**   I know the name, of course, but I've never met him.

**Chris Richter**   He's a great boss – I'm his PA. How about you?

**Sam Isaakson**   I'm an accountant in the finance department.

**Chris Richter**   Finance? This must be a busy time of year for you!

**Sam Isaakson**   Yes, the busiest – we're closing the accounts for the year.

**Chris Richter**   Actually, I'm quite busy at the moment, too, as we've got our annual company trip next weekend, and I'm responsible for organizing everything. It's a nightmare!

## 26.1

**Masako**   So, welcome to Kyoto, Sue, Heather.

**Sue**   Thank you very much. This is a wonderful city, really.

**Masako**   Is this your first time here?

**Sue**   No, I was here with an Australian trade delegation five years ago. What about you, Heather?

**Heather**   First time for me, I'm afraid.

**Sue**   So, Masako, Heather, what have you two been doing since Vancouver last year?

**Masako**   After you, Heather.

**Heather**   Well … I've been learning Spanish …

**Sue**   Really?

**Heather**   Oh yes, and I've been decorating my house all by myself, and I've been doing a lot of jogging. Can't you tell?

**Masako**   Yes, you've lost weight, haven't you?

**Heather**   I sure have. How about you, Sue?

**Sue**   I've finally finished my doctorate.

**Masako**   Oh, well done, Sue.

**Heather**   That's fantastic.

**Sue**   Thanks. It was about time! And, what else? We've been looking for a house to buy, but prices are so high these days.

**Masako**   Oh yes, here too.

**Sue**   And for the last few months I've been helping my daughter a lot with her studies. She wants to start university next year. But anyway, Masako, what have you been doing?

**Masako**   Well, not much. I've been working too much, … and I've got married.

**Sue**   What? Oh, that's wonderful news! Congratulations!

## 26.2

**Carlton**   Good to see you again, Ku-duk, Miguel. How are you keeping?

**Miguel**   Fine.

**Ku-duk**   Not bad. And yourself, Carlton? How was your trip from San Francisco?

**Carlton**   I don't know, I slept all the way. What about your flight from Costa Rica, Miguel?

# listening script

**Miguel** Very long, but I caught up with some reading. Now I know what I have to say when I give my talk tomorrow. But that's enough about me. Ku-duk?

**Ku-duk** From Seoul it's only about one and a half hours. I hardly had time to sit down. So what have you both been doing since last year?

**Carlton** After you, Miguel.

**Miguel** Well, it's been a very busy year at work.

**Carlton** Oh, come on, don't talk shop!

**Miguel** OK, OK. I've become a father.

**Carlton** Finally! Hey, congratulations, Miguel!

**Ku-duk** Yes, that's wonderful!

**Miguel** And, as you can imagine, I haven't been sleeping very much since he was born. But I've been taking a lot of photos of him. Ku-duk, what have you been up to?

**Ku-duk** Me? I've been doing a course in traditional calligraphy for six months, and it's going well. It's fascinating really.

**Carlton** Yes, maybe you could teach us if we can't agree on how to manage climate change!

**Ku-duk** And I've been giving my classes at the university, as usual. And what's new at your end, Carlton?

**Carlton** Oh, a lot of travelling, lobbying, you know, politics, to get the funding for research projects, that sort of thing. And ... I've been learning Russian.

**Miguel** Why Russian?

**Carlton** Well, I've ... er ... I've met ... er ... someone who's ... er.

**Miguel** Ah ha ...

**Ku-duk** And how long have you been learning Russian for, Carlton?

**Carlton** Well, only for three months.

**Miguel** So tell us something in Russian, Carlton.

**Carlton** Nyet!

## 27.1

**Joanne** So, David, have you ever had a frightening experience on a plane?

**David** Sort of. A couple of years ago I was flying from Athens to Tokyo – I was living in Greece at the time, and a friend of mine who was working in Japan had invited me to stay with her. I flew overnight from Athens and had a short stopover at Bangkok – just long enough to have a walk around the airport. While the plane was getting ready to take off, there was a sudden flash in one left-hand side engine.

**Tom** A flash of light, or like an explosion?

**David** A flash of light, no noise, no flames. And the plane carried on moving. Apparently, the pilots hadn't noticed, but a lot of the passengers were starting to panic. They were getting up out of their seats, calling out to the cabin crew, who also hadn't seen anything, apparently.

**Joanne** And what did they do, the cabin crew?

**David** They told the pilots, and a few seconds later the plane came to a halt. We had only moved a few metres. And then outside the plane it was suddenly like a disaster movie – you know, flashing lights, sirens, people running around. It was incredible! Some of the passengers were shouting to be taken off.

**Joanne** And were you panicking?

**David** To tell you the truth, I continued reading my book. I mean, there was nothing I could do. About ten minutes later, they evacuated us off the plane and drove us to a five-star hotel in Bangkok, and gave us a room to rest in, and food. Later – the food, by the way, was out of this world – anyway, later, at three o'clock in the morning, we were called to reception to get onto buses.

**Joanne** How long had you been there?

**David** About ten or twelve hours. Anyway, we boarded the same plane, and yes, most of the passengers were quite frightened as it started to taxi. But after that we had no further problems, so we finally got to Tokyo about seventeen hours late.

## 28.1

### 1

**A** Hello how are things? What's your new boss like? How's she getting along?

**B** Really well! It was the right choice to appoint somebody from outside the company. She's so enthusiastic. She's got everybody working well, she keeps us motivated and you know how important that is in our place! It's important that she's goal-oriented too. She always lets you know exactly what she wants to do, which is great! Now you know exactly where you're going and what you have to do. She's good at meetings too. She makes everyone contribute. She's got all of us making suggestions and coming up with ideas. It's not easy to find someone so enthusiastic. Great, everyone's really pleased!

### 2

**C** How are you getting along with the new manager?

**D** Fine, she's a good listener all right. She seems to be quite open-minded – she hasn't got fixed ideas. She listens to you and wants to know what you think about things. She lets you develop your ideas if she thinks they're good. And then she's very practical and direct about things. She said that she doesn't expect results immediately but she doesn't allow anybody to waste any time. I think everybody is happier than before. She makes you want to do a good job. Everyone seems to get along with her quite well.

### 3

**E** Hi! How's work?

**F** Oh not too bad. Did you know we've got a new boss?

**E** No I didn't. Since when?

**F** Since last month. He's new to the company.

**E** What's he like? Is he difficult to work with?

**F** I still don't really know. He certainly knows his job, but he can be quite single-minded about reaching targets and things. At the first meeting we had with him, he wouldn't allow us to change anything. He seems very ambitious as well. He's got us all talking about profit margins and money. He's making us work all right, but at least you know where you are with him.

### 4

**G** What's the new manager like? Has he made a good start?

**H** Oh yes, I think he has. I mean he's really charming. He makes everybody feel respected and important at work. You know that we have had problems in the office with so many different characters and we used to have arguments all the time. Well, that's all changed now. He definitely knows what he wants to do but he seems to be quite easy-going. If you've got a problem, he just listens and then he lets you do things in your own way. He's good at dealing with conflict and he never gets angry or loses his patience with anyone. No, very good. I think you made the perfect choice!

## 29.1

### 1

**A** Hi, Susan. I was wondering if you'd like to join us for a drink later. We're going to the Irish pub.

**B** Sounds like a nice idea. I'd love to, thanks. It's time I met my new colleagues.

**A** OK, then. We're meeting outside at eight.

**B** That's great. See you there, then.

**2**

**C** Right. Well, this summary of your ideas looks very interesting.

**D** Oh, um. Shall I make you another copy? It won't take a moment …

**C** Er, no, actually. There's no need. I've got a copy at the office. But thanks, anyway.

**D** Right, fine. Anyway …

**3**

**E** Any chance of you coming out on Saturday? Helen's coming over. We're all going out for a meal.

**F** Helen? Is she here? Oh, I wish I could come, but …

**E** Oh, you can't make it? That's a pity!

**F** No, I'm afraid I can't. I'm away at a wedding. If only it was next weekend. Oh well, thanks anyway! Next time, perhaps.

**4**

**G** So how are you feeling? When's your speech? You've still got half an hour, haven't you?

**H** Yes. But, um well, I've never given a talk in front of, of so many people before.

**G** Well, would a drink help? Can I get you a brandy perhaps?

**H** Oh, I wish I could have one! But I'd better not. It's fine, thanks.

**G** OK, well I'll get you some water.

**H** Oh, that's kind. Thanks.

**5**

**I** Well, it's really time I went … oh, it's raining again!

**J** Do you have an umbrella?

**I** I wish I did!

**J** Oh, do you need a taxi?

**I** Well, I'd rather walk. But, yes, that's kind of you. A taxi would be great. Thanks.

**J** OK. I'll just give them a call.

**6**

**K** OK. Well we'll start with the snails. Tim, you'll have some, won't you? They come in a wonderful garlicky sauce with lots of French bread.

**L** Um er, well …

**K** I'm sure you'll like them. They're a speciality here. You must try them.

**L** Well, actually, I'd prefer to have something simple to start with. Um, maybe I'll have just a salad.

**K** Oh. That's such a shame! Oh, go on, Tim.

**L** No really. It's quite all right. Thank you.

## 29.2

**1**

**A** So, I guess we'd better go. Great party, yeah? Oh – can I give you a lift?

**B** Well actually … um..

**A** I'm going your way. It's easy, really.

**B** No it's OK. There's no need. I'll ask John, or maybe walk.

**A** Oh. OK.

**2**

**A** Right. Any chance of you coming with us to a nightclub?

**B** No, I'd better not. I'm rather busy from nine tomorrow.

**A** Oh, go on! I know a place right next to your hotel!

**B** Really? OK then, well just for one drink. Thanks!

## 30.1

**Mandeep** Hello, Torrent Airline Catering. Mandeep Bains speaking.

**Jackie** Good morning. This is Jackie Westinghouse from Northern Airlines. May I speak with Lee Pheng?

**Mandeep** I'm afraid he's just left –

**Jackie** Just left? Oh no! I've been trying to get through to him all day.

**Mandeep** Pardon me, what did you say?

**Jackie** Can you give him a message?

**Mandeep** Sure.

**Jackie** Well, the thing is, our computer system has been shut down for some technical reason, and you're not going to be able to log on to our database until our engineers sort it out. Since we depend on this for exact passenger numbers and dietary requirements, this will affect flights from Singapore to San Francisco the day after tomorrow.

**Mandeep** Sorry, but could you speak more slowly please? This information's important so I need to get it down clearly.

**Jackie** Oh. Sure.

**Mandeep** I didn't catch your name.

**Jackie** Jackie Westinghouse.

**Mandeep** Is that Wastinghouse?

**Jackie** Westinghouse, with an 'e' for echo.

**Mandeep** OK.

**Jackie** So, anyway, I have details on the individual passengers here, and I'm going through them to get the information we need. As soon as I have the numbers, I'll fax them over. Are you with me?

**Mandeep** I think so.

**Jackie** So, the database problems affect NOA 576 departing Singapore to San Francisco at 09.45 on Sunday, and NOA 1145 leaving at 22.30 also the day after tomorrow.

**Mandeep** Sorry, I don't quite follow. Sunday is tomorrow, not the day after tomorrow.

**Jackie** Sorry, here in the States it's Friday. Time difference!

**Mandeep** I got you.

**Jackie** So that's all the details. Could you read them back to me?

**Mandeep** Yep. NOA 576 at 09.45, and NOA 1145 taking off at 22.30.

**Jackie** Hang on – was the last time three-zero or one-three?

**Mandeep** Three-zero.

**Jackie** That's fine then.

**Mandeep** I'll pass that on to Mr Lee as soon as he gets back.

## 31.1

**Receptionist** National Builders' Association. Can I help you?

**Della** Good morning. My name's Della Wilson from A&G Construction. I don't know if you can help me but I'm organizing a conference about Health and Safety at Work and I'm trying to find someone who could give a talk about the new safety standards.

**Receptionist** Excuse me, but I'll put you through to PR. They'll be able to help you better than I can. Hold the line please!

**Della** Yes. Thank you.

**Suzanne** Public Relations, Suzanne speaking.

**Della** Good morning. My name's Della Wilson from A&G Construction. I'm organizing a conference about health and safety at work, in the building sector to be more precise, and I'm trying to find someone who could give a talk at the conference. Is this the right department or should I …

**Suzanne** Did you say the building sector?

**Della** Yes. That's right. It's about safety at work. I'm interested in speaking to someone who could give a talk about the existing safety standards in the construction industry. Do you know who I need to speak to or what department could help?

**Suzanne** Just a second. I'm just thinking which department … 'safety in the building sector'? Yes. I think you should speak to the Inspections Department. I'm sure they'll be able to help.

**Della** Thank you. Could you put me through then please?

**Suzanne** Sorry, I can't do that from here. I'll put you back with reception. Just a second!

## 31.2

**Receptionist** National Builders' Association. Can I help you?

**Della** The Inspections Department please.

**Receptionist** Just a second. I'm putting you through now.

**Man** Inspections Department.

# listening script

**Della** Good morning. My name's Della Wilson from A&G Construction. I was directed here by your PR department. I'm organizing a conference about health and safety at work in Liverpool at the end of this month and I'm trying to find a person who could give a talk about the recent changes in the safety standards in the building sector.

**Man** For the end of this month you said?

**Della** Yes. I know it's very short notice but one of the speakers has just cancelled so I need to find somebody else.

**Man** Well. You've got the right department and I think we can help, but probably you should speak to Peter James. He often gives talks at conferences.

**Della** Peter James. Good.

**Man** Just a second. I'll see if he's available. Don't hang up!

## 31.3

**Peter** Peter James speaking. Can I help you?

**Della** Good morning Mr James. I have just been speaking to a colleague of yours who said I should speak to you. My name is Della Wilson from A&G Construction. I'm organizing a conference about health and safety at work in Liverpool at the end of this month and I would like to know if you would be interested in giving a talk about the recent changes in the safety standards in the building sector – I believe you know a lot about the subject. The talk would be for about an hour, including question time. We think about 100 people are coming.

**Peter** Sounds interesting. But the end of the month you said? No. I'm afraid I'll be very busy then, so I doubt I'll be able to make it – in fact, I'd better say no. Sorry!

**Della** That's OK – I understand. I'd really appreciate it if you could recommend someone else, though. It's a very important subject. I mean the number of accidents is going down slowly but …

**Peter** Yes. Listen. Why don't you speak to my colleague, Alastair Wilkins? He's an expert on the new safety standards. He's probably the best person to talk to, in fact.

**Della** Oh good. Could I speak to him now?

**Peter** Just a moment … Hello? It appears he's not in his office right now … ah, now I remember – he's visiting a building site this morning. If you like, I could give him a message when he comes to work tomorrow.

**Della** Well, I was hoping to find someone this morning.

**Peter** Well. In that case you could try his mobile. I'll give you his number.

**Della** That would be wonderful, thank you.

**Peter** It's 564 770808.

**Della** 5 6 4 7 7 0 8 0 8.

**Peter** I hope he'll be able to do it. Tell him that you have been speaking to me and that I gave you his number.

**Della** Yes I will, and thank you very much. You've been a great help!

## 31.4

**Alastair** Alastair Wilkins speaking.

**Della** Good morning. My name's Della Wilson from A&G Construction. I got your number from Peter James, who said that you might be able to help me.

**Alastair** Sorry? Could you speak up a bit please? There's a lot of noise here.

**Della** Yes. My name is Della Wilson from A&G Construction. I spoke to your colleague Peter James this morning and he gave me your number. The reason I'm phoning is that I'm organizing a conference about health and safety at work. It's in Liverpool at the end of this month. It's the last Friday of the month. I'd like to know if you would be interested in giving a talk about the recent changes in the safety standards in the building sector. Of course we will pay all your expenses and everything. The talk would be for about an hour, including question time. About 100 people are coming. Do you think you could help?

**Alastair** In Liverpool? … Hang on … well, I'm looking at my diary, and it looks like I'm free that day, so I should be able to do it … I don't think I'm doing anything at the end of the month, but, listen, there's too much noise to speak here. Could you phone me at the office tomorrow morning and we could talk about all this in more detail?

**Della** Yes, of course.

**Alastair** You have the number?

**Della** Yes. Can I phone you at around 10.00?

**Alastair** Could you make it a bit later? I'm meeting some people at 9.30. Say about 11.00?

**Della** Yes. 11.00 is fine. Thank you ever so much Mr Wilkins.

**Alastair** Please, call me Alastair. I'll look forward to our conversation tomorrow. Thank you for calling. I'm afraid I have to go now. Bye!

## 32.1

**Kristina** Van Deer Cheese, Amsterdam. Kristina Van Deer speaking.

**Rosie** Hello Kristina, this is Rosie Elder from Mission Bay Delicatessen in New Zealand.

**Kristina** Hello, Rosie, good morning. It's evening there in New Zealand, I suppose.

**Rosie** Yes, it is. How are you?

**Kristina** Busy, you know what it's like at this time of year, don't you? How are things?

**Rosie** Can't complain. Listen, I'm phoning to order this time because …

**Kristina** Let me guess … You haven't been having some problems with a computer virus, have you?

**Rosie** Yes, we have. Gordon, I told you!

**Kristina** OK. Let me take this down. I suppose you wanted some Edam, didn't you?

**Rosie** Yes, that's right, send me four boxes of mature Edam if you can, and five of young Edam.

**Kristina** No problem. I've got plenty of stock.

**Rosie** And I'd like to place an order for Gouda: three large, and nine small.

**Kristina** OK for the large, but we've only got six boxes of small Gouda in stock at the moment. Would you like the rest later?

**Rosie** No, we'll take those half dozen and forget about the rest. Now, have you got stock of low-fat Gouda?

**Kristina** Not until next month.

**Rosie** Never mind, then. And I wanted, … Let me see … Two boxes of North Holland extra mature.

**Kristina** Anything else?

**Rosie** And can you give me four boxes of large Maasdam?

**Kristina** Can you wait until next week for those? We're a bit low on stock.

**Rosie** OK, but the rest will be ready for shipping in about two days, won't it?

**Kristina** Yes, in two days. You should have it there in about a week. It's the usual terms of payment, isn't it?

**Rosie** Yes, the same as ever.

**Kristina** And you're still at the same address, aren't you?

**Rosie** Yes.

**Kristina** Anything else?

**Rosie** No, that's all for now.

## 32.2

**Rosie** No, that's all for now.

**Kristina** OK then. Now, could you re-send the order when your email is working properly? I need it for the export papers.

**Rosie** Did you hear that, Gordon! Right, Kristina, let's go through the order now, shall we?

**Kristina** Sorry, what was that?

**Rosie** Shall we just check those numbers? I just want to double-check everything.

**Kristina** So that's four boxes mature Edam, five boxes young Edam, Gouda: three large, six small. Plus North Holland extra mature: two boxes. That's everything, isn't it?

**Rosie** Yes, apart from the four boxes of Maasdam. How long will they take?

**Kristina** They should be in at the start of next week. So that's twenty-four boxes to go now, four next week.

**Rosie** I make it twenty-four boxes too. Thanks, Kristina. Bye.

**Kristina** Thank you, Rosie. Nice doing business with you. Bye.

## 33.1

**Jeff** Jeff Clark, Sales.

**David** Hello Jeff. This is David. Thanks for sending me the letter for Paul Howick.

**Jeff** No trouble!

**David** Yes but there are one or two changes that I'd like to make before we send it off.

**Jeff** OK! Just a sec! I've got it here on the computer. Yeah. Go ahead!

**David** Well, I think it's just a little too informal in places. Look at the first line. Could you put 'I'm writing to thank you' instead of just 'say thanks'?

**Jeff** Sure. 'I'm writing to thank you for your fantastic …'

**David** No, just a second. Could you change 'fantastic' to 'kind'? I think that sounds much better.

**Jeff** Good! … OK?

**David** Yes, and please delete the reference to lunch at the end of the sentence. It was excellent, but I don't think we have to mention that here.

**Jeff** All right! So the first line's 'I'm writing to thank you for your kind hospitality … etc.' Is that right?

**David** Yes. In the second sentence in the first paragraph, could you change 'great' to 'most impressive'?

**Jeff** 'Most impressive' … OK. Anything else?

**David** Yes. Look at the beginning of the second paragraph. Just 'we want' sounds very informal. Change the beginning to 'We would like to invite you …'

**Jeff** Just a minute … 'We would like to invite you' … OK?

**David** Yes. There's a spelling mistake in the same line. The name of the assistant is Davis, that's d-a-v-i-s, not d-a-v-i-e-s.

**Jeff** Oh, but it sounds the same, doesn't it?

**David** Yes, but we must be very careful with people's names. In the same line I'd like you to change the word 'factory'.

**Jeff** And what do you want me to put instead?

**David** I think 'facility' sounds better.

**Jeff** Good. Is that it?

**David** No, just two more changes. Delete the last sentence and write 'Could you please let us know when would be convenient for you?'

**Jeff** OK … 'Could you please let us know when would be convenient for you?'

**David** … and, finally, change the 'Best wishes' to 'Yours sincerely'. After all, I don't know him that well.

**Jeff** OK. Shall I read that back to you?

**David** Yes, please. I'd like to send it off this afternoon.

## 33.2

**Janet** Janet speaking.

**Phil** Hi Janet. This is Phil. Have you got a minute?

**Janet** Yes. I suppose you're phoning about the order form.

**Phil** Yes, I am. Have you a had a chance to look at it?

**Janet** Yes. I did it this morning. Have you got it in front of you?

**Phil** Yes, I've got it here.

**Janet** OK, it's much better than the last one but I've thought of several changes.

**Phil** All right. Go ahead!

**Janet** Well, in the words 'Order Form', the typeface is a bit too big. Make it a little smaller. And you see where you've put the company logo?

**Phil** Yes?

**Janet** Well I think it would look much better in the top left-hand corner of the page, right at the top, and you could put the words 'Order Form' just under the logo. That would look a lot better.

**Phil** OK. It would save space too.

**Janet** Yes. And I wouldn't use colour for the logo. Just the black and white version.

**Phil** Why's that? It'd look a lot more attractive in colour.

**Janet** Yes but think of the printing costs. We have to make thousands of these!

**Phil** Yes, I suppose you're right.

**Janet** OK. Now the lines where you have the details of how to order with our phone number and everything. Can you see that? At the top of the page?

**Phil** Yes, what's wrong with that? I haven't put the wrong phone number, have I?

**Janet** No. But I think you should put these four lines at the bottom of the page.

**Phil** You think so? OK.

**Janet** Now I know that this is just a draft version, but I really think it's easier for people to fill in boxes than to write on a dotted line. So put boxes where you have all the dotted lines. And don't forget to put eight boxes for the customer number. That way they won't forget a number!

**Phil** Good idea! Anything else?

**Janet** You could do the same for where they have to write their email address in the middle of the form.

**Phil** I don't know about that. Some people have really long email addresses.

**Janet** You don't think we should change the email line then?

**Phil** Erm … No, I think it's OK. Let's leave it.

**Janet** OK then. What's next … just a moment. Ah! The next one is … Yes. It's difficult to read the note about the credit card address. Can you make that a lot bigger? It's very important. We're always having problems with this.

**Phil** Perhaps we could add the letters 'NB' in big letters before the credit card address. Write it in the left-hand margin so it stands out.

**Janet** Yes, that might help.

**Phil** OK I'll do it … NB … Good, that's useful.

**Janet** Just one more thing. Can you see the last two columns in the order form on the right-hand side of the paper?

**Phil** Page number … catalogue code …

**Janet** No, on the other side of the paper. Right. The ones that say 'Individual price' and 'Total price'?

**Phil** Oh, yes. Sorry.

**Janet** Well, I'd suggest dividing each of these columns into two. One for pounds and one for pence. Make it easier for people to fill it in and it might be less confusing for us!

**Phil** Good. Anything else?

**Janet** No, that's all I could think of. I'm sorry if I've given you a lot of work!

**Phil** No, that's fine. You've been a great help. I'll make those changes and send you the new version. OK?

**Janet** Good! Bye for now!

**Phil** Bye, Janet, and thanks …

## 34.1

### 1

**Receptionist** Ealing Taxis. Can I help you?

**John** Good afternoon. Yes, I have a problem. I phoned for a taxi for four o'clock and it still hasn't arrived and it's now twenty past. This is the longest I've ever had to wait!

# listening script

**Receptionist**  I'm sorry about that sir! Could I have your name please?

**John**  It's Harris, John Harris.

**Receptionist**  Is that 14 Draycourt Gardens? To Liverpool Street Station?

**John**  Yes that's right.

**Receptionist**  Just a moment Mr Harris … Mr Harris? Your taxi is on its way. There are roadworks on the A211 and the driver says he's never seen such a traffic jam on that road. But he'll be there in five minutes.

**John**  Great – thanks for that. It's not your fault. I'll be waiting outside the house.

## 2

**Receptionist**  Fastpost Services. Good afternoon. Can I help you?

**John**  Yes. Good afternoon. I'm phoning from Harris and Jones Ltd. Yesterday, we asked you to deliver some documents in Manchester this morning before ten. Your express delivery service.

**Receptionist**  Yes, sir.

**John**  Well the problem is that the documents didn't arrive until this afternoon, at three o'clock, in fact. I mean, this is very frustrating, because our client did need them this morning.

**Receptionist**  That's very strange, sir.

**John**  It is. I specifically asked for special delivery and your office guaranteed delivery before ten.

**Receptionist**  Do you have a reference number?

**John**  Yes, it's 3/W12.

**Receptionist**  Mr John Harris, Harris and Jones Ltd, 24 Blackburn Street?

**John**  That's right.

**Receptionist**  Just checking, sir. Oh. I don't understand this, but your documents were sent by normal delivery – that's a next-day service.

**John**  But you've obviously made a mistake. We made it perfectly clear that we wanted the express service. Your courier knew that when he picked the documents up from our offices, and my secretary told your office on the phone.

**Receptionist**  Yes sir, you're right. There's been a mistake somewhere.

**John**  Well, you will of course modify the invoice for this delivery. I don't want to have to pay any extra.

**Receptionist**  Yes of course, Mr Harris. I'll do that immediately. I am sorry about all this.

**John**  And could you please make sure that this sort of thing doesn't happen again?

**Receptionist**  I certainly will. I've never heard of such a thing happening here before.

**John**  Well, it's not the first time we've had this problem.

**Receptionist**  Don't worry, Mr Harris. I'll speak to the manager about this.

**John**  Thank you. Goodbye!

## 3

**Receptionist**  ISO Camera Centre.

**John**  Good morning. My name's John Harris. I left my camera, a Yoshida, for repair last month. Do you know if it's ready?

**Receptionist**  Just a second, sir. The name was …?

**John**  Harris – John Harris.

**Receptionist**  Just a second … Here we are. John Harris. A Yoshida Hotpix 70x. Is that right?

**John**  Yes.

**Receptionist**  Well I'm afraid it isn't ready, sir. We couldn't repair it here, so we had to send it to the technical centre in Luton.

**John**  You had to send it …

**Receptionist**  Yes. They say it'll take about a month to repair.

**John**  Another month! That's impossible!

**Receptionist**  It's the normal time for repairs like this, sir.

**John**  But you can't seriously expect me to wait for another month. I'm going on holiday soon and I need my camera. No. No. Another month is simply out of the question.

**Receptionist**  I am sorry about this, sir, but there's nothing I can do.

**John**  Well, could I speak to the person in charge or the manager or somebody?

**Receptionist**  I'm afraid the manager isn't here just now.

**John**  In that case, could you give me the manager's name and could I have your name as well? I'll be making a formal complaint in writing about this. I've never had such poor service before!

**Receptionist**  The manager will be here tomorrow morning, sir. You might want to phone then.

**John**  Yes. I will. I'm sorry to go on about it, but this is totally unacceptable. Tell the manager I called, please.

**Receptionist**  Yes I will, sir.

## 40.1

**Sarah**  Hello, Sarah speaking.

**Mike**  It's Mike here, Sarah, from Marketing.

**Sarah**  Hello, Mike. What can I do for you?

**Mike**  Could you make some travel arrangements for me?

**Sarah**  I'll try. What do you need?

**Mike**  I've got to go to the States at the end of next month for a couple of meetings …

**Sarah**  Let me just jot down the dates and everything.

**Mike**  I've got an all-day meeting in Boston on the 27th, so I'll be needing flights and accommodation.

**Sarah**  Right. I'll get back to you later.

## 40.2

**Lucy**  Four Seasons Travel. Lucy speaking.

**Sarah**  Hello Lucy, this is Sarah from DSL Graphics. How are you?

**Lucy**  Can't complain. How can I help you?

**Sarah**  I need return tickets and accommodation for my colleague, Michael Wise, going to the USA next month. Can you get me a flight to Boston on the 26th, and the return flight on the evening of the 27th or on the 28th?

**Lucy**  … to Boston on the 26th, return flight 27th pm or the 28th … Do you know what hotel he wants to stay at?

**Sarah**  At any hotel that's central but not too expensive.

**Lucy**  Any preferences for airlines?

**Sarah**  Yes, the cheapest.

**Lucy**  Let's see … Manchester to Boston, departing 09.15 arriving in Boston 15.15 local time. That's with a stopover at Newark. OK. Shall I book?

**Sarah**  Yes.

**Lucy**  Boston to Manchester on the evening of the 27th … nothing direct. Through Washington at 22.50 … is full, but there's one on the 28th, departing 10.00 arriving Manchester 20.15. Is that OK?

**Sarah**  Mmmm, the 27th would be better, but anyway.

**Lucy**  I'll put him on the waiting list and see.

**Sarah**  OK. Let me know when you have the hotel sorted out, will you?

**Lucy**  OK, I'll call you back in a while. Bye.

## 40.3

**Sarah**  Sarah Thorpe speaking.

**Lucy**  Hi Sarah, this is Lucy from Four Seasons Travel. I've got those flights confirmed for Mr Wise.

**Sarah**  Great. Can we just go through them?

**Lucy**  He's flying on BLE flight 466 to Boston via Newark on the 26th, departing Manchester 09.15 arriving at Boston at 15.15 local time. Now on the 28th he flies back on EZL 195, departing at 10.00 and lands at 20.15 at Manchester Airport.

**Sarah**  That sounds fine. What about the accommodation?

**Lucy**  In Boston he'll be staying at the Liberty Inn on the 26th and 27th. I'll be emailing all the prices to you this afternoon.

**Sarah**   That will be great. Thanks a lot, Lucy. Bye.

…

**Mike**   Marketing. Hello.

**Sarah**   Hello, Mike. I've got your business trip sorted.

**Mike**   Brilliant. Let me just get a pen … OK.

**Sarah**   You're flying on Monday 26th on BLE flight 466, departing from Manchester at 09.15 and arriving at Boston at 15.15 local time. OK? You'll be staying at the Liberty Inn for the two nights. Then on the 28th you fly back, departing at 10.00 and you're back in Manchester at quarter past eight in the evening. How does that sound?

**Mike**   Sarah, didn't I say it was Baltimore?

**Sarah**   What?

## 41.1

### 1

**Paolo**   Good evening. I have a reservation.

**Receptionist**   Good evening. What name is it, please?

**Paolo**   Carbalho. Paolo Carbalho.

**Receptionist**   How long are you staying, Mr Carbalho?

**Paolo**   I'm staying for two nights.

**Receptionist**   OK. You're in room 312 on the third floor. Here's your key card.

**Paolo**   Ah. How does this work?

**Receptionist**   Well, once you've opened the door, you have to insert it into the slot in the wall to turn on the electricity in your room.

**Paolo**   Right. And does it also activate the air-conditioning?

**Receptionist**   Yes. The air-conditioning comes on as soon as you put the card in the slot.

**Paolo**   Fine. Do you think you could give me a wake-up call tomorrow morning?

**Receptionist**   Yes, certainly. What time?

**Paolo**   At seven o'clock, please.

**Receptionist**   Of course.

**Paolo**   And what time is breakfast?

**Receptionist**   Breakfast is served from seven to ten, and lunch from twelve until two.

**Paolo**   Right.

**Receptionist**   Do you need any help with your luggage?

**Paolo**   No, it's all right thanks. I can manage. Could you tell me where the lift is?

**Receptionist**   Yes, it's just at the end of the passageway. Enjoy your stay at the Imperial Hotel, Mr Carbalho.

### 2

**Paolo**   Good morning. I'd like to check out, please.

**Receptionist**   Good morning, Mr Carbalho. Did you enjoy your stay?

**Paolo**   Yes, the room was very comfortable. I'm afraid I have a problem with the remote control for the television, though. It fell in the bath last night while I was getting out, and it doesn't appear to be working now. I'm terribly sorry.

**Receptionist**   Don't worry, Mr Carbalho. We'll sort it out. Thank you for telling us. Did you have anything from the minibar?

**Paolo**   Yes, I had one bottle of mineral water and some beer.

**Receptionist**   How many bottles?

**Paolo**   Just one. And I also made two telephone calls to Lisbon.

**Receptionist**   Right. I'll just add that to your bill. That's €354.25, please.

**Paolo**   Can I pay by American Express?

**Receptionist**   Yes, of course.

**Paolo**   Here's my card.

**Receptionist**   Thank you. Could you sign here, please?

**Paolo**   Of course. Would it be OK to leave my bags here? My plane doesn't leave until later this afternoon, and I want to do a bit of shopping before I leave Ljubljana.

**Receptionist**   Yes, certainly. Just bring them into the office, and you can leave them as long as you like.

**Paolo**   Thank you. I'll be back at about three o'clock to pick them up.

## 42.1

**Jun**   So let's just check where the Opera House is. Can you get out the map?

**Wei**   I thought you had the map! Never mind – let's ask, shall we?

**Jun**   No need – I'm sure I can remember the way. So, if I remember right, we're supposed to go down the far end of Hyde Park. Then we go through that gate and into … er … What was it … Maguire Street?

**Wei**   Macquarie Street!

**Jun**   How come you're so good at names? He said we should keep going right to the end, until we get to the harbour.

**Wei**   Logically. Let's get going then.

## 42.2

### 1

**Wei**   Now where were we meant to be having lunch? The Harbourside, wasn't it? Hi there. Excuse me, is this the right way to The Harbourside? It's a restaurant. It's supposed to be easy to find but …

**Neil**   The Harbourside? OK, you go back down here and when you get to Circular Quay, turn right. That's Alfred Street, and you carry on to the end. Have you got that?

**Jun**   Sorry, was it right or left at Circular Quay?

**Neil**   Right.

**Jun**   OK, and then what do we do?

**Neil**   Then you take the first right again – that's George Street – and keep walking. You can't miss it.

**Wei**   That's very kind of you.

**Neil**   You're welcome. Bye.

### 2

**Wei**   I thought men were meant to have a good sense of direction!

**Jun**   I'm sure they told us in Centrepoint that it was down here.

**Wei**   I think maybe we were supposed to stay on that main road, and not turn right. I'm going to ask anyway. Excuse me, is Chinatown in this direction?

**Pippa**   Er …

**Wei**   Am I right in thinking we go straight down this road first?

**Pippa**   Yes, you go straight on until you get to Kent Street, and it's third on the right.

**Wei**   So that's second right into Kent Street, then third right.

**Pippa**   You've got it. Go down there, take the second right.

**Wei**   Thank you – you've been very helpful. Bye.

**Pippa**   Yeah, bye.

**Jun**   OK, you're not meant to cross over here, but let's do it anyway.

**Driver**   Watch where you're bloody going!

**Jun**   Why do these people drive on the wrong side of the road?

**Wei**   Maybe they think we do.

## 43.1

### 1

**Carlos**   So, where shall we go?

**Bill**   Well, there's a nice little Italian place not far from here. Otherwise, we could be a bit more adventurous. There's a new Vietnamese restaurant. I was there last week. It was excellent.

**Carlos**   Well, Bill, if you think it's a good choice …

**Bill**   Yes. I think you'd like it.

…

**Carlos**   So, Bill, what do you recommend?

**Bill**   Well, Carlos, the stir-fried lamb with mint and chilli is good. I had that last time. Or there's lamb in a hot garlic sauce. It's served with rice.

**Carlos**   Well, it all certainly sounds different.

**Bill**   Vietnamese food often has lime and mint in. And you'll always get lots of noodles too. Maybe you'd like to try the fish?

**Carlos**   No, no. I think I'll go for one of the lamb dishes. The one with mint.

business **one** : **one**     127

# listening script

**Bill**  Right. And I'll have the chicken in lemon grass, I think. Anything else?

**Carlos**  No, that's fine for now.

**Bill**  OK. I'll catch the waiter.

**2**

**Eva**  This is a very cosy place. That's the good thing about these bistros: they've got a nice family atmosphere too. And look – all those jars of pickles, and dried fruits. It's just like someone's home!

**Amy**  Oh, I love it here because it's so European. I come at least once a week. And they have an excellent wine list. Anyway, what will you have?

**Eva**  Er. Well, I'd like something quite light, you know, not too spicy.

**Amy**  And vegetarian, right?

**Eva**  Yes, I'm afraid so. I haven't eaten meat for years now.

**Amy**  Well Eva, you really should try the Greek vegetable dish they do, then.

**Eva**  Oh yes, what's that?

**Amy**  Well, it's a plate of grilled eggplant, tomatoes, and zucchini, with goat's cheese. It's delicious.

**Eva**  Well that sounds very nice. And what are you having, Amy?

**Amy**  I think I'll have the roast goose. It comes with steamed red cabbage and boiled potatoes. Mmmm my favourite! And, er, do you want anything before?

**Eva**  No, nothing to start with, thanks.

**Waiter**  Good evening, ladies. What can I get you to drink?

**Amy**  Hi. Well, ah, a dry white wine. Erm … a bottle of this pinot grigio, please, and, er, some mineral water?

**Eva**  Yes, sparkling for me, please.

**Amy**  And one still.

**Waiter**  OK. I'll be right back.

…

**Amy**  Well that was really good. How was yours?

**Eva**  Very nice. They're friendly here, aren't they? Oh, some more wine?

**Amy**  Well, just a drop. Thanks. Would you like a dessert? The chocolate cake is really rich – it's just so good!

**Eva**  No, really, I couldn't. That was fine.

**Amy**  Well maybe we could share one?

**Eva**  Er, does it have nuts in? I'm allergic to nuts.

**Amy**  No, but it's got alcohol in.

**Eva**  Oh, OK, then!

…

**Amy**  Could we pay please?

**Waiter**  Certainly.

**Amy**  Do you take cards?

**Waiter**  Of course.

**Eva**  Let me do this.

**Amy**  No, no, I insist. This one's on me!

## 44.1

**1**

**Taxi company**  City Cabs, hello.

**Mr Hansen**  Hello. I'd like a taxi please.

**Taxi company**  Your address?

**Mr Hansen**  Oh, um it's in Clifton, and, er, Cedar Avenue, number 252, Cedar Avenue, Clifton.

**Taxi company**  Er, whereabouts is that?

**Mr Hansen**  It's right in the middle of Clifton. A few hundred metres along from the Royal Crescent.

**Taxi company**  And your name?

**Mr Hansen**  Er, … Hansen.

**Taxi company**  And where are you going to?

**Mr Hansen**  I'm going to The Oasis Restaurant. It's just to the north of the town centre, out towards the airport.

**Taxi company**  It'll be about twenty minutes waiting time, I'm afraid.

**Mr Hansen**  Oh, that's OK. I'll wait. Thank you. Goodbye.

**2**

**Driver**  Mr Hansen?

**Mr Hansen**  Yes, that's right. I'm going to um … the Oasis Restaurant.

**Driver**  Right. Um. OK. The Oasis, you said? Is that in the centre of town?

**Mr Hansen**  No, it's a little way out of town. It's on the way to the airport, a few kilometres from the centre.

**Driver**  Ah, right. I think I know where you mean.

…

**Mr Hansen**  Right, it must be somewhere near here … Oh yes, it's over there, I think, after the next set of lights. You can see the business park on the left, and The Oasis is just on the other side of that, just a few hundred metres down the road. I'll tell you when we're near. We're not too far now.

**Driver**  Right. OK. That's fine.

**Mr Hansen**  Right. Um, you can drop me here if you like. The restaurant is just over there.

**Driver**  Oh, OK then.

**Mr Hansen**  Could I have a receipt please?

**Driver**  Certainly.

**Mr Hansen**  Oh, and er, keep the change.

## Listening bank 01

**Interviewer**  Most of us have access to a PC these days, either at home or at work, but how many of us are happy with the way our computer looks? Even the newest state-of-the-art laptops issuing from the main hardware companies lack character in their design, despite the fact they're becoming slimmer and more sophisticated. As a reaction against this lack of originality on the part of computer manufacturers, an increasing number of people have started to change their machines themselves in a new craze known as 'modding', a term taken from the English word 'modify': to change or adapt. These 'modders' as they are referred to, think up a design, get out the toolbox and the paint and create a completely unique machine. Some choose to change their computer into a zebra by spray-painting it with black and white stripes. Others add an extra fan to help cool the CPU down, some add coloured light displays, and a few even go as far as to install their apparatus in a machine designed for a completely different purpose: the range runs from motorbikes to coffee machines. Dirk Stein is a modder and he's with us here in the studio today. Dirk, who first thought up the idea of modifying computers?

**Dirk**  I don't really know who the first modder was. I think modding, sort of, came about by accident. Someone tried to make their computer run faster (that's called overclocking) and then they discovered it started to overheat. So then they had to add a fan, which looked a bit old-fashioned, and so they started to design cooling systems for computers. All this made it necessary to change the shape of the CPU case to incorporate the new accessories. And after putting the case back together again, you obviously have to repaint it, so people started experimenting with colours and patterns. By adding a window and some lights the design became even more special, and that's how modding was born.

**Interviewer**  I've heard there are even modding competitions now, Dirk. And you're thinking about entering one of these, is that right?

**Dirk**  Yes, I've got a pretty good idea for the next case mod contest run by ExtremeTech, but I can't tell you exactly what I'm going to do, or that would spoil the surprise.

**Interviewer**  Tell us about the contest, Dirk.

**Dirk**  Well, first you have to design your mod and then find all the parts you need, which is the hard bit. When you've built your mod, you have to take three photos and send them in, together with a 300-word description about why you think your mod is interesting. The competition organizers take about six weeks to decide on a winner, and they send you your prize, which last time was a complete PC modding kit.

**Interviewer** Can you tell us about some of the winning designs from previous years.

**Dirk** Yes, the winning designs have been absolutely crazy. The winner of last year's contest, which had a science-fiction theme, managed to build his computer complete with a desk into a TIE fighter from the film *Star Wars*. It looked incredible, especially at night, because the whole cockpit was lit up by red lights.

**Interviewer** So you're giving us no clues on what your mod might be then?

**Dirk** All I'm going to say is if the theme next year is fantasy mods, I think I've got a fairly good chance of winning.

**Interviewer** Well, Dirk, thank you for talking to us and good luck with the competition next year.

Now, Todd Buckingham of XXX, what's behind this modding craze? Why are people buying perfectly good computer equipment and then investing time and even more money changing its appearance?

**Todd** Well, first of all, modders don't just change the appearance of their computers, they also change the way they work, but it all boils down to the same thing. Computer fanatics are bored with the same old designs that are on offer, and so they're taking matters into their own hands. If the manufacturers don't come up with more innovative designs, then the people at home are capable of creating them for themselves. The IT world is one which is always changing, but at the moment the industry is not keeping up with the users' demands.

**Interviewer** So do you think modding could have a long-term effect on the computer industry?

**Todd** Well, the companies that continue producing the same old designs will eventually go out of business. It's as simple as that. Only the manufacturers who listen to the demands of their customers for innovation and originality will survive into the future, and even some of the big names in the industry may be lost.

**Interviewer** Todd Buckingham, Dirk Stein, thank you very much for talking to us.

## Listening bank 02

**Interviewer** Do you ever wonder what would happen if you gave up your job, sold your house, and moved to a quiet spot in the country? Well, it seems that people all over the world are doing just that, in a trend known as 'downshifting'. Dr Ivan Schwarz of Schwarz & Co. Market Research, what kind of people are willing to give up a financially comfortable lifestyle in favour of a lower income and less stability?

**Ivan Schwarz** Well, just because a family has opted for a lower income doesn't mean to say that their situation is unstable. The key is to find a simpler lifestyle so that you have time to do what you want to do, while still remaining financially viable. Dropping out of society completely does not enter the equation.

**Interviewer** Thank you for clarifying that, but, tell us, what type of people make this kind of decision? I mean, we all talk about the consumer society and how important it is to everyone to have a nice house, a new car, the latest technology in your living room, etc. Are there really people who reject this?

**Ivan Schwarz** Yes, there are, and, in fact, there is a growing number of people who believe that time is more important than money or possessions. First of all, you've got your fifty, sixty-year-old who is heading for retirement and has already secured a reasonable pension and can afford to step back and reduce their working hours. Then you've got the loyal employee who is laid off in their late forties and would like to do something more rewarding with their life, and so invests their redundancy pay in a small business, such as running a guesthouse in the country. And finally, you have your couple in their thirties who have just had a child or two and are fed up with not being able to spend time together as a family, and so decide to look for a much more rewarding life on a lower budget.

**Interviewer** Dr Schwarz, you've talked about people looking for a better quality of life. Is this the main reason why families are downshifting?

**Ivan Schwarz** It's definitely one of the reasons, yes. The most common reason for downshifting is to spend more time with family, but a desire for a healthier lifestyle, more personal fulfilment and a more balanced lifestyle are also important. In some cases a life-changing event, like a death in the family or a marriage break-up, may also start people thinking about the meaning of life and cause them to investigate the possibilities of downshifting. In general, it's the need to exchange a stressful, high-speed lifestyle for a more enjoyable, balanced life.

**Interviewer** So, can you give some advice to those of our listeners who would like to quit the rat race in order to pursue a lifelong dream?

**Ivan Schwarz** Well, the most important thing is not to make any changes to your life without first planning your finances in advance. You will not be happy in your new situation if you have to worry about how you are going to pay your mortgage. It might be necessary for you to sell your house and buy a smaller one, or you may have to take up a part-time job until your gardening hobby turns into a successful small business. Whatever happens, you have to be prepared to face cash-flow problems, and this is always easier if you have planned effectively beforehand. This will be the biggest problem over the first twelve months or so.

**Interviewer** OK. So, I've planned my finances, I've put my savings away to cover the first year. What should I do next?

**Ivan Schwarz** If you have friends or family who have downshifted, get ideas from them. If you are planning a move to the country, get to know the area before you actually sign for your new property. Prepare your family for the move and involve all of them in the decision to remodel your life. That way they won't blame you if things go wrong.

**Interviewer** Thank you, Dr Ivan Schwarz of Schwarz & Co. Market Research. Now we've got Helena Shipman in the studio with us. She downshifted from a highly paid position in a management consultancy in the capital, and now runs a dog behaviour clinic. Helena, can you tell us why you decided to make such a radical change to your life?

**Helena Shipman** Well, I started finding it really hard to get out of bed in the morning, and I found I just wasn't motivated enough to get to work on time. So I mentioned the idea of me giving up work to my husband, and we started talking about things we could do to change the situation.

**Interviewer** Your husband works from home, doesn't he?

**Helena Shipman** Yes, he's a graphic designer, so he's very flexible about where we live. We both wanted to move to the country, so we spent a lot of time at weekends looking for a nice place to set up our new life. It took a long time, but I'd advise anyone to do it. You don't want to jump in with both feet.

**Interviewer** So your husband could work from home, but then you had an office job, didn't you?

LB02

# listening script

**Helena Shipman**   Yes, that's right and that's what my husband said too. He knew I'd be happier with some meaning in my life in the form of a job.

**Interviewer**   So, why the dog clinic?

**Helena Shipman**   Well, we'd always had dogs at home when I was a child, but living in a flat in a big city, I didn't think it was fair to keep one shut in on its own all day. The kids kept pestering me for one as well, so I enquired after a course on dog psychology, which I found on the Internet, and spent a year studying for my diploma. So now I'm a qualified dog psychologist, and people come to me to sort out their difficult pets.

**Interviewer**   And are you happy with your new life?

**Helena Shipman**   Yes, I've never looked back, to be honest with you. We're not as well-off as we used to be, and my husband has to help out more with the kids, but our quality of life has improved tenfold. I really recommend downshifting to anyone who has that early morning stomachache when their alarm goes off, even if they only decide to reduce their working hours. It's great to see so many people turning away from materialistic values in search of a more satisfying life, and I'm so glad to be part of that.

**Interviewer**   Dr Ivan Schwarz, Helena Shipman, thank you for talking to us.

## Listening bank 03

**Interviewer**   So, how long have you been in business?

**Ian**   Well, we started in this particular business thirty-four years ago. My father had just been made redundant, and the owner of this shop was retiring, so he basically sold it to us. Dad finished his old job on the Friday, and moved into this job on the Monday. In the beginning, my Dad looked after the fish, and my uncle did the greens. Then later my uncle retired, so we bought him out.

**Interviewer**   And how many staff work here now?

**Ian**   There are seven full-time staff, and a driver on deliveries. And we have four part-timers for Fridays and Saturdays. Saturdays can get really busy.

**Interviewer**   What about the range of produce?

**Ian**   We try to get as wide a variety as possible. In the fish range, shellfish is big. And we have fresh chicken brought in five days a week. In the game season we have pheasant, duck, rabbits, …

**Interviewer**   And where do you get them from?

**Ian**   Well, most of the fish is from Scotland or Cornwall, but we obviously get tuna and swordfish from overseas, usually from Oman and the Philippines. Rabbits and pigeons are usually locally shot around Cheshire and North Wales. The venison and chicken are local too.

**Interviewer**   Generally, who are your customers?

**Ian**   A very wide range, actually. Locals pop in for something cheap and easy to cook, such as fish kebabs. Mothers come, trying to get their kids to eat fish. The middle-aged of course have always eaten fish. And older people come in too. So we've a great customer base. We've been on a number of television cooking programmes recently, and we're also on a few websites, which has really increased trade. The public have more confidence to cook with fish nowadays. I'd say eighty or ninety per cent of our customers come in knowing exactly what they want, and they're full of ideas as to how they want to cook it. But for those few who don't know, then our staff can help out and give advice on two or three alternatives. People love that, and find it very impressive. We're always discussing ideas, and asking our customers how they cook things, and then passing that on to other customers.

**Interviewer**   What about competition over the years?

**Ian**   Well another fish shop opened just up the road in the early nineties. We thought people would be loyal to us, but it wasn't like that. It was all quite interesting, really. But overall it's made us better at business, and made us examine what we do. For example, before, people were getting fish full of bones, so we started offering to skin and bone them. That was popular. And then we did the same with salmon, whole salmon, and people were delighted. We also started offering all kinds of other useful little services – we can lend the customers special cooking equipment, for example, or we can cook a lobster for them. We also prepare crab, so that it's cooked and ready to eat from the shell.

**Interviewer**   How have you coped with the new supermarkets?

**Ian**   Well, we thought it would be a disaster for us, but nothing seemed to happen. It's just increased business. You see, the locals round here aren't short of money, and this particular retail store, a multi-million pound business with an excellent reputation for produce, thought it was a good idea to open up. Soon after it was clear that it was helping us too. You see, it's very difficult for a supermarket to provide its customers with quality fish and game. We're such a one-off shop that there isn't actually much competition. Apart from the quality produce we have, we don't pre-package our food. The customer comes in and gets what they ask for, just as they want. And if we vacuum-pack it for them, then they can freeze it in large quantities, and just take out enough for one meal at a time.

**Interviewer**   So what have you done to make sure the business remains successful?

**Ian**   Well, we try to keep up with the times and improve the look of the business and the shop. We put in air-con, and we're always updating such things as scales, refrigeration, and vac-packing machines. We make sure we always stock a good variety of produce, and all the time we try to get the best quality fish, to find the best possible source of fish at a fair price, so that we can charge a fair price to the customers. To attract new customers, at special times of year, for example, at Christmas or during the barbecue season, we place adverts in local magazines – although word of mouth is the way most of our customers hear of us.

**Interviewer**   Do you think people spend more on good fish and meat these days?

**Ian**   Absolutely. They might think twice before they buy it, but at the end of the day people forget the price, and always remember the quality. And when they eat it, it's exactly what they want!

**Interviewer**   Indeed. Well, thank you very much.

## Listening bank 04

**Interviewer**   Good evening – welcome to tonight's programme. We begin with a short quiz. Are you ready? Can you answer the following four questions? But first I should tell you that there is only one correct answer to all of them.

Which company has more than 50,000 different product lines? Sells more than $1,344 every second? Has operating profit margins of over 30%? Has achieved all this in just ten years?

Do you know what company we're talking about?

If you haven't guessed by now, it's called eBay. As they say themselves, it's the world's online marketplace, and one of the most successful companies on the

Internet today. More than 400,000 people earn all or at least a considerable part of their annual income through eBay. This evening, we take a close look at the company and try to find out what makes this company so unique and so successful.

We spoke to Jack Wallace, head of e-commerce studies at the New York company of B2B Consultants. Jack – eBay is about to celebrate its tenth anniversary. I understand that it all started in a very small way.

**Jack**  Yes, that's right. It was set up by Pierre Omidyar in 1995. Pierre was a computer programmer who decided to design a database on the web to help his wife in her hobby. She needed a way of getting in touch with people who had the same hobby. It all started from there. The page was immediately popular and people started selling many different articles. In the first six months they had handled 10,000 operations. That's when they decided to give up their normal jobs and develop eBay into what it is today.

**Interviewer**  It's been estimated that more than 10% of all the time that British people spend on the Internet is spent on eBay. What makes it so popular?

**Jack**  That's right – and they spend more money on eBay than they do on going to the cinema. I think there are several reasons for its popularity. For a start, eBay is exactly what it says it is – it's the world's biggest marketplace. If you consider the number of people who access eBay, either to sell or buy something or simply just to browse through what's on offer, then eBay is like an enormous street market, full of different products all with one very powerful attraction, which is that they usually cost considerably less than in traditional shops.

**Interviewer**  With the added advantage that you don't need to leave your home.

**Jack**  Exactly! A virtual marketplace.

**Interviewer**  Which means that people can also sell from their home as well.

**Jack**  From their home or from their normal business. Don't forget that many 'normal' shops have an eBay site where they can sell their goods to a much bigger market. But it is fundamentally comfortable. I mean, we all like walking around street markets – so it's only logical that we enjoy walking around a virtual market offering more than 50 million different items, from the comfort of our own home.

**Interviewer**  But not all the articles on sale are second-hand, are they?

**Jack**  No, in fact a lot of the things you can buy are completely new or at least unused. But of course there are more second-hand items for sale. I mean we all have things in our house or office that we never use, just taking up space. That old computer, the camping equipment that we never use now, a present that somebody gave us and we don't really want, and so on. There are market studies that show that the average house contains more than $3,000 in articles that are never used. eBay offers you an easy and fairly safe way of selling them.

**Interviewer**  So you can tidy up the house and earn money at the same time. That's a very simple and attractive concept. But eBay now has more than 147 million registered users. How has it managed to grow so much in such a short time? Especially when you consider the number of dotcoms that haven't done so well in the same period.

**Jack**  Probably the real strength of eBay is the very professional management team that runs the company. Meg Whitman, the CEO, has been running the company for several years now and she's built up a very strong team. She came to eBay with a wealth of business and marketing experience in leading American companies. Did you know that the magazine *Business Week* has included her on its list of the twenty-five most powerful business managers in the USA, every year for the last four years?

**Interviewer**  So the secret is the original concept and the management team …

**Jack**  Oh yes, but we shouldn't forget that the eBay site is very well-designed and extremely easy to use. In that respect it's probably one of the best sites on the web. That makes it popular for the average Internet user who doesn't want complications.

**Interviewer**  How easy is it to pay for things on eBay, and how safe is it?

**Jack**  Good question. Payment security is still a problem on the Internet. This is still one of the reasons why many online companies or dotcoms still haven't taken off. Lots of people are worried about using their credit card on the Internet. They don't like giving their personal details to someone they don't know, but I think this mentality is changing very quickly.

**Interviewer**  Yes? Why do you think that?

**Jack**  Well I think we're getting more and more used to paying for things with our credit card, and people are using online banking services more and more. We all know about passwords and security systems and, if we follow the rules, it's really a safe process. Many eBayers, er, … people who use eBay, have an account with PayPal, which is a secure system of paying for things online by credit card and this works very well. I can't remember the exact figure now, but I think it's something like 72 million people have opened an account with PayPal.

**Interviewer**  That's more customers than a large bank! But another question that many people often ask is the other aspect of security. How can you be sure of getting what you're paying for?

**Jack**  That's another good question. But before I answer, let me tell you an interesting anecdote about eBay. About a year after Pierre Omidyar had set up the company, he wrote an open online letter to all the registered users. In those days, there were about 50,000 people. In this letter Omidyar said that eBay was based on one fundamental understanding. That people are honest. It might sound a bit innocent but that's the way it is. eBay is based on honesty. OK. OK. Of course there are problems and the occasional case of fraud, but if you consider just how many different transactions there are on eBay in a single day, then the number of these cases is very small indeed. Obviously eBay knows that this is one area that they have to control very seriously, which they do. And then there's the feedback system to help you.

**Interviewer**  Could you say something about how that works?

**Jack**  Well, fundamentally, it's a system of personal recommendations or criticisms from the people who use eBay about the other people on eBay. When you buy or sell something you are asked to leave a comment on the person you have bought something from or sold something to. This is known as the Feedback Comment – right now there are more than 3 billion recorded feedback comments on eBay. Before you buy or sell something to a person, you should look at what other people have said about them. If they pay on time, describe the article fairly and accurately, communicate well, and send things quickly, and so on. Sometimes, especially if the article is expensive, you might need to have a certain number of positive feedback comments before you can participate in the auction.

LB04

# listening script

**Interviewer** How do you see the future of eBay? Do you think it can keep up its present rate of growth?

**Jack** I think it will continue to grow but at a slower rate. So far we've just been speaking about individuals buying from other individuals. In fact, there are hundreds, no, thousands of small businesses on eBay. We call them online shops. These could be existing shops that use eBay to supplement their sales or shops that only exist on eBay. I think we will see more and more of these virtual shops opening up. After all, it only costs about nine euros a day to have a shop on eBay. You don't need to make a big investment at all.

**Interviewer** But you have to pay a small fee or commission on everything you sell.

**Jack** Yes, but it is a very reasonable fee, and don't forget that the first thirty days are completely free for those who would like to try it.

**Interviewer** Well, thank you very much, Jack. That was very interesting. I hope we'll have the chance to discuss eBay again with you in the future.

**Jack** Thank you. It was my pleasure.

## Listening bank 05

**Interviewer** So, Gemma, tell me a bit about your company.

**Gemma** We organize and coordinate weddings in Spain. About 95% of our weddings are in the Barcelona region, though we've occasionally done weddings in other parts of Spain. Broadly speaking, there are two main areas to our work: the first is organizing the wedding, the venue, and finding suppliers, contracting all the people you need, and …

**Interviewer** Sorry, who do you mean by that?

**Gemma** Well, everyone, from the caterers, the car or minibus hire people, the hairdressers, the manicurist, the florist, the people who make the cake, musicians, the photographers if they want them …

**Interviewer** Don't all couples want photographers?

**Gemma** No, they don't actually. It depends on what they contract – often they'll be happy for friends to take photos. They're never as good, but it's a way of cutting costs, and well, this brings us to all the budgeting side of things. Then the other area, which is really important of course, is coordinating of the big day itself. That's as important – if not more important – than all the planning.

I suppose our role on the day of the wedding is like Jennifer Lopez in the film 'The Wedding Planner'.

**Interviewer** How long have you been in operation?

**Gemma** My partner and I set up the business in 2003 and since then we haven't stopped working.

**Interviewer** How are Spanish weddings different from other countries'?

**Gemma** The Spanish really spend a fortune on their wedding, and even if it's a humble family, they'll often take out a bank loan to be able to have their dream wedding. And because of our Latin character, we tend to throw weddings where it's a bit like a show – I mean the waiters making a grand entrance with the plates in time to music, you know, marching to music and flashing lights. And you have waiters handing over bouquets of flowers to the mothers for all their hard work in the preparations and so on. And the bride walks around all the tables with her bouquet of flowers in time to music, and when the music stops she has to give the bouquet to the nearest girl who hasn't got a partner …

**Interviewer** Who hasn't got a partner?

**Gemma** Yes, so that she'll find a boyfriend soon!

**Interviewer** I see!

**Gemma** Then there's music for the presentation of the wedding cake, and there's often singers and musicians during the ceremony and at the meal. And there are two little figures of a bride and a groom on the wedding cake, and they get given to the next couple who are getting married. You know, it's basically a huge party with everybody chanting. And especially plenty to drink. And having a bar where the guests can drink as much as they like is a must at a Spanish wedding.

**Interviewer** Sounds good to me. Now, what kinds of things can go wrong?

**Gemma** Normally the problems happen on the wedding day, the unforeseeable ones. We have lots of stories to tell about these, ones that nobody could foresee that we've had to solve. I don't know – there was one recent wedding when the bride's mother – she was a bit of an amateur florist – had insisted on doing her daughter's bouquet herself, as well as all the flowers for the men's buttonholes, and with all the nerves on the wedding day she forgot to put

the pins in the buttonholes, so they couldn't attach the flowers to the men's lapels. It …

**Interviewer** So how did you sort that one out?

**Gemma** It was easy, because we always carry an emergency kit where we have pins and safety pins, and things like that.

**Interviewer** Oh yeah, what else?

**Gemma** Well, let me think – a first-aid kit, aspirins, paracetemol, stain removers, safety pins – let's see – deodorant, perfume and cologne, a sewing kit, buttons. What else? Quite a bit of make up, dental floss, moisturizing cream, a sponge for cleaning shoes, scissors, sellotape, a hairbrush, oh, and batteries and a battery charger. And superglue – very handy in a crisis.

**Interviewer** I'm amazed.

**Gemma** There was another case with the lapel flowers. All the flowers arrived at the hotel at 4 p.m., one hour before the wedding, and when I checked everything, I saw that the lapel flowers weren't there. I rang the restaurant where the meal was going to be to find out if they'd got mixed up with the flower arrangements for the tables, but they weren't there either. The groom was in the hotel lobby chatting to his friends and family, about to go to the church and we had no flowers for him! I phoned the florist and – can you believe it? – they wanted us to go there and pick up the flowers! There was only half an hour to go to the ceremony and no time to get to the florist and back anyway. I sent one of our staff on a motorbike to the flower kiosks in the town centre and I told the groom that my assistant would be waiting for him at the church with his buttonhole – his lapel flower – and that's how it turned out. We had the flower waiting for him at a quarter to five when he arrived. We put it on him and no one was any the wiser. But it was all very stressful for us.

**Interviewer** Any problems with transport? You know, wedding cars and taxis?

**Gemma** Erm, once – the driver of the hired coach got the wrong address to pick up the guests. He was waiting at one place and they were waiting at another – two hotels with very similar names – and we were getting worried because the ceremony was due to start in twenty minutes. The companies never give us the drivers' private mobile phone numbers. So we phoned the company and told them it was an emergency, and they gave it to us.

**LB05**

So we were able to give him the right address, and he got the guests to the church with two minutes to go. There are hundreds of anecdotes like that, but they always turn out well so long as there's someone who knows what they're doing, who knows what is supposed to happen on the wedding day. The bride and groom know they don't have to worry because they know we'll be there to deal with the problems.

**Interviewer** And what are the things that you most like about this work?

**Gemma** What I most like about this work is seeing the look of happiness on the couple's faces when everything turns out the way they want. Or when the families congratulate us on the good organization, I mean that's really nice ... I suppose helping a couple to have the wedding of their dreams, something that will be one of the happiest days of their life – that makes me feel good.

**Interviewer** What qualities do you need for this job?

**Gemma** Lots of patience, because you have to deal with couples who are about to get married and require a lot of attention. They can get very tense, and their mothers ... What else? Good organizational ability – it's a very delicate job, where, if you're not organized, it can all get chaotic. You have to be a bit of a perfectionist, everything has to be just right, down to the last detail. You can't afford the luxury of making mistakes. Lastly, an ability to resolve problems fast. On the day of the wedding, unpredictable things can happen and you have to fix them without the bride and groom realizing that something has gone wrong, and then getting upset. Our aim on the day is to make sure the couple enjoy the day, and aren't aware of any slip-ups.

**Interviewer** And finally, any advice for couples on their wedding day, or for a happy marriage?

**Gemma** It's a very happy day and the couple should enjoy their day. Hire good professionals and you'll be able to enjoy the day with no worries. Savour the day – yes, savour it. Find some time to sit down for five minutes with your partner over a glass of champagne and watch how the day is unfolding. Enjoy it – it's over quickly. There are no secrets for a happy marriage: every couple is different, but, in general, I'd say that you should never lose respect for your partner, and of course good communication is a must. Everything is easier when communication is fluid.

## Listening bank 06

**Interviewer** This morning we're interviewing Nicky Pritchett-Brown, Sponsorship and Development Director of the Edinburgh International Festival. Nicky, you're the Sponsorship and Development Director. What exactly is your role?

**Nicky** Well, I look after fund raising from business and from trusts, as well as from individuals. I do this for the Edinburgh International Festival, which is one of the most famous arts festivals in the world. At Edinburgh, we try to push back the boundaries and aim to present performing arts that couldn't easily be presented by anyone else. It can be anything from opera, theatre, and dance, both classical and contemporary, to concerts with a solo performer or a whole orchestra. These artists wouldn't be performing elsewhere in the country during the season, at least not with the same programme.

**Interviewer** How long has the festival been running?

**Nicky** After the war, in 1947, a group got together wanting to encourage people to feel more confident about the future and to get better understanding between international people, something that would help the 'human spirit flourish'. There are stories from those early days of Russians walking down Princes Street. People from all over came together. So we use the arts to try to develop understanding between different peoples. And unlike many other festivals, with our significantly cheaper ticket prices, we can cater to all people – the rich, music lovers, as well as those exploring the arts for the first time. But of course to supplement box office revenues, we also need both public and private sector funding. And it's the private sector funding that I'm responsible for – for developing collaborations and raising money with corporate entities: businesses.

**Interviewer** How do you go about getting a sponsor?

**Nicky** We are very fortunate because we already have strong relationships with a number of important businesses who have sponsored the festival over a number of years. The Bank of Scotland, for example, claims to have supported the festival since the beginning in '47, but other companies have been involved for very many years too, and see the benefits of the festival not only for their own business purposes, but also for the economy of Scotland, and the importance of the arts for a healthy economy, and healthy society.

**Interviewer** How do sponsors benefit, in tangible terms?

**Nicky** Working with our business partners, we put together a package of benefits to fit their needs. So there'll be a package of tickets included in the deal plus the option to buy more tickets at a discount, or for their staff. On tickets, programmes, posters, adverts, any promotional activity we do, we'll credit our sponsors, so there's immense publicity for them too. You see, it actually makes a difference whether we get sponsorship or we don't, as to whether we can afford the performance or not. Without our sponsors, there'd be no festival. We're very proud of the associations we have with them. We have a launch party in March with them when everything is announced, and then we usually have a lunch on the first day of the festival on the Sunday, and that's specifically for the funders and sponsors to come along. We also regularly have an event in the autumn to thank all those who have been involved.

**Interviewer** Where does this money come from? Why do companies want to sponsor the festival?

**Nicky** Well, for some it's from their marketing, or sponsorship budget, or even their corporate social responsibility budget. They enjoy an association for many different reasons. It could be for their own corporate entertainment, although that's less prominent than it used to be. Or the companies might be looking for an association with excellence, an association with something of quality that matches their brand. For example, Renault Espace let us use their cars, you know those 'people carriers', to ferry artists around during the festival, from the hotel to the performance venue. Renault's target market are people who we'd expect to see at the festival. Another reason for sponsoring might be for investment into the community. One firm in this category is Scottish and Newcastle, who have their headquarters in Edinburgh, but they have businesses round the globe. Obviously, it's vitally important when doing new deals in, let's say, Russia and China, that when they talk about their headquarters, Edinburgh is seen as an international city. So it's about raising potential clients' confidence in the company.

**Interviewer** Do companies choose to sponsor a particular event?

# listening script

**Nicky** Yes. We're always looking for a situation where a sponsor and the project they are sponsoring are compatible. It's crucial that both parties understand what the other wants. They may choose a brand new commission, which can be quite risky, or something more familiar and more reliable, maybe some classical chamber music. But it's crucial that the sponsor is working with a project that is appropriate to what they want.

**Interviewer** What do you mean by risk?

**Nicky** Well, there could be nudity, bad language, or topics that are 'difficult' and yet contemporary and relevant. The company Standard Life, for example, who deal with investments, life assurance, and so on, wanted to update their image, tell the public that they are an 'interesting and contemporary' company. So they chose to sponsor something completely new and unknown, a Catalan theatre piece, that also involved film. Well, once people started to see it, they just thought it was absolutely sensational. It completely sold out. That was a few years back now, but although Standard Life have sponsored other projects since then, this year we've finally managed to get the same theatre company back with another new work, with Standard Life sponsoring it. They're delighted. But of course, again, as it's never before been seen in the UK, we're ready to expect the unexpected!

**Interviewer** With such an international appeal, do you find there are any cultural issues to bear in mind?

**Nicky** Oh, all the time. But we work very hard to understand what the requirements of the artists are, and that those requirements are matched to the sponsor. For example, a few years back we had some Indian musicians performing, and it was only when they arrived in town that they said they needed a huge Indian carpet to sit on. We're talking about the stage of Usher Hall here. It's enormous! Well, I walked round the corner to the nearest carpet shop, had a very nice chat with the owner over a cup of tea, and managed to do a deal on this most fantastic carpet. We borrowed it in exchange for some credits in the programme and a few tickets. So it was really a tiny sponsorship, but it made a huge difference to the artists to have a nice Kashmiri carpet to sit on. It was an example of one of those things where you think, you know, 'how on earth are we going to manage', and ultimately I think it's a real tribute to how the people who live and work in Edinburgh see the festival as something important, and they are happy to be involved. Normally, I can't believe this guy would lend a carpet. It must have been worth thousands of pounds. But he saw the fun of being associated with the festival and so was happy to do the deal. It was his largest carpet.

## Listening bank 07

**Interviewer** ... and now for the final report in today's programme of *Business News* in which we visit one company that has managed to solve some serious problems with a very innovative building design. Delta Call Centre Services was set up in 1996 in south-east London, and quickly became one of the leaders in the sector. By 2001 the company employed over 150 people but, as Michael Burton, personnel manager at Delta told us, despite its success, the company had to find answers to some very serious problems.

**Personnel manager** We were doing well, but we had one fundamental problem – we were losing staff too quickly. Our staff rotation a few years ago was over 60% a year, with people staying just over six months on average.

**Interviewer** And what were the reasons for that?

**Personnel manager** I think the main reason was the high level of stress that the job has. Our most important activity is sales promotions – trying to persuade people to buy things – and phoning three to four hundred people in a single day can be very stressful. The job can also become very repetitive – you start phoning people at 9.00 and you follow the same script, the same basic conversation, all day. It can become quite tiring. Furthermore, you have the additional pressure of reaching your targets.

**Interviewer** And this high turnover of staff obviously had knock-on effects ...

**Personnel manager** Well, obviously, if staff leave, then you have to replace them. We were recruiting new people all the time. This was not only expensive, but it was difficult to find the right sort of person with the right qualities. When we found them we had to train them. It takes about six months of training and hands-on experience to get used to the job, and we were constantly starting new training courses and forming new work teams. And you can't keep morale high when people are constantly leaving.

**Interviewer** But now Delta has a staff rotation of less than 5% a year and you were voted as one of the ten best companies to work for last year, so you obviously found a way to solve these problems. How did you turn things round?

**Personnel manager** All the managers sat down for a couple of days and looked at every aspect of the working conditions. We started to realize that the actual physical conditions were at the heart of the problem. The offices were in a dark, old building, with just enough space to seat everyone in front of computers – nowhere to relax or to meet colleagues. We knew that if we wanted to continue growing, we desperately needed to change the physical surroundings.

**Interviewer** So it was felt that the solution was to design and build new offices.

**Personnel manager** Yes, and that gave us the opportunity to completely rethink the way we were working, and look at ways in which people's physical surroundings were connected to their level of happiness and motivation.

**Interviewer** You opened your new building three years ago.

**Personnel manager** That's right. We now employ more than 250 people. As people are working for us longer, we've been able to cut our recruiting and training costs dramatically. I receive up to fifty letters of application and CVs a month.
...

**Interviewer** I'm about to enter the Delta building with Susan Hartley, the architect who designed it. What did Delta ask for?

**Architect** It was quite a challenge. Delta's employees are mostly young, fresh out of university or college, and they wanted a building they would really like to go to in the morning and which would stimulate them.

**Interviewer** And what you came up with is really quite unusual. To get here we've walked through a park with a small lake. You cross a little bridge and walk in ... There's a lot of light through the glass roof ... We're in a large open space with small coffee areas and sandwich bars which is more like a village square than a modern office building.

**Architect** We wanted to make people feel relaxed as soon as they walk in, to help minimize the feelings of stress and pressure that had been a problem.

**Interviewer** This ground floor is not just a social area, though.

**Architect** No, in fact most of the meetings at Delta are held in the entrance area. When people feel relaxed, we believe they communicate more effectively, and feedback from Delta's managers supports this.

**Interviewer** You have designed the other two floors in different styles, with three completely different environments and atmospheres. Let's go up to the first floor.

…

**Interviewer** So here on the first floor is the centre of operations.

**Architect** Yes. The first floor is divided into six big open areas for the call centre teams. We decided to use open offices to help promote teamwork. They can all see each other, but it doesn't feel crowded at all. As you can see, everyone uses mobile headsets so they can get up from their desks and walk around the office, so they don't get bored just sitting at their desks. They can stretch their legs and look at the view outside.

**Interviewer** So very different from the cramped conditions before.

**Architect** It certainly is. Depending on the type of call they are making, we believe it's better to be able to stand up and walk around while you're on the phone. Delta has told me that the number of calls each employee deals with in a single day has increased by around 15%. The views, the natural light and the open space all contribute to a relaxed and happy atmosphere, which is especially useful when dealing with a difficult customer. And they don't experience the sense of isolation you can have when you can't move around or even see your colleagues.

**Interviewer** People are smiling more than I'd expect in an office, certainly. One reason for this, so I hear, is the top floor.

**Architect** Let's go and see that.

…

**Interviewer** So this is the social area. The first thing I see, taking up about a third of the floorspace, is what appears to be a social club.

**Architect** Delta felt that social facilities are extremely important to young people, so we created this based on research among staff – the design is actually based on an Irish pub, as these are popular with young people.

**Interviewer** It's very lively in here. I can see people chatting, listening to music, playing on the games machines, using the Internet …

**Architect** The company encourages the staff to take frequent short breaks because they know this helps productivity. It's very much 'their place', if you see what I mean. I think it helps them identify with the company, and feel it belongs to them. It makes them feel good about working there, and it definitely has a positive effect on team-building in general. Delta also organize regular parties here as a reward.

**Interviewer** What about the rest of the top floor?

**Architect** Let's take a look.

…

**Architect** This is the health club – with an aerobics gym, weights room, and a sauna. People come here early in the morning before work, or at midday or to unwind after a busy day on the phone! You can get rid of all the tension that's been building up during the day, which means that you can be fresh for work the following day. It's open all week, except on Sundays – it's one of the things that makes the company hard for employees to leave.

…

**Interviewer** I'm talking to Jennifer, who's been working at Delta for three and a half years. How have things changed for you at Delta?

**Jennifer** I've made a lot of friends since we moved here, and we even spend a lot of time here after work, which would have been unthinkable before. Also, I've been promoted several times, so the money is obviously better. Now that people stay longer, they start to think of working here as the first step in a career rather than just a temporary job.

**Interviewer** But for the ordinary worker, the job is still the same, and that can be stressful.

**Jennifer** True, especially if you're on selling – that's why the breaks are important, so you don't allow stress to build up. And so that the work doesn't get too repetitive, they've organized it so that people work on the same project for a couple of weeks and then move onto something new. It's easier now to change round the people in the teams more frequently because we know each other so much better. Because everything is all open, we know how we all work and also we want to work hard for each other because we're friends.

**Interviewer** And the most productive team each month gets to have a party.

**Jennifer** Yes, that motivates us too.

**Interviewer** Michael Burton … This was an ambitious project. Three years on, what's your verdict?

**Personnel manager** Oh everybody's delighted! It was a huge investment, but we now have a much more settled and happier workforce, more permanent teams and much higher individual productivity. In our business it's important to give a positive and cheerful image when you're working on the phone and we're sure the building helps us to achieve that. Morale has never been higher.

**Interviewer** Delta now employs 250 people and won one of the Best Company To Work For Awards last year. The building cost over eight million pounds but it seems to have been money very well spent!

## Listening bank 08

1

**Interviewer** So, Bill, can you tell me what you do, please?

**Bill** Sure. My name is Bill Newson. I live in Auckland, in New Zealand and I'm a trade union organizer.

**Interviewer** So what do you actually do, as a trade union organizer? What does your work involve?

**Bill** Well, trade unionism is like a political calling really. It's something I commit my life to. Unionism is essentially organizing workers in their workplaces into collective groups to take advantage of their collective bargaining strength. About 20% of New Zealand workers are members of trade unions.

**Interviewer** Can you say something about your daily routine?

**Bill** Sure. I'm like a manager within the union and I have thirty field staff who operate out in the workplaces across Auckland and the surrounding region. My job is to make sure that they're attempting to achieve the objectives of the union in the workplace. So I do a lot of work by mobile telephone and we operate a lot via email. Essentially, they contact me if they have problems, and I contact them to make sure they're getting on with their job.

**Interviewer** What sort of problems occur?

**Bill** Well, OK … unionism is about representing workers in issues with their employers. So, for example, we can be negotiating a collective contract for better wages or workplace conditions. Or there might be a disciplinary situation where an employee has been given a warning or even dismissed from their job. There's a whole range of different issues around that general theme.

# listening script

**Interviewer** Do you find that because of the nature of your work, you're in situations of conflict very often?

**Bill** We're in conflict all the time. Essentially, trade unionism comes from a political philosophy that there are two forces in the workplace and society: capital and labour. Now, some political philosophies hold that they are in conflict all the time, because capital is trying to get the best return for the investment, and labour is trying to get a bigger share of the cake. But conflict has many different varieties and shades.

**Interviewer** And conflict can come from outside the company too, can't it? So what major issues are happening right now in New Zealand?

**Bill** I suppose the big issue is, given that we've grown our economy, at what point should we reward workers for contributing to that?

**Interviewer** What do you mean exactly?

**Bill** In New Zealand our economy has been doing quite well for a number of years, and so the big issue is to try and get a greater share of the cake, in terms of better wages for our members. So we'll be running a big campaign to increase wages above what the trend has been in recent years, and we've done a lot of research to justify that campaign. We've already started some talks with the central employers' groups, and they're going to be vigorously defending themselves against a significant pay rise.

**Interviewer** Wow, so you're under a lot of pressure. It must be tough, but, on the other hand there must be rewards too – what do you like about your job?

**Bill** I really love my job. I think the most enjoyable thing is – all of the thirty field staff that I work with, and the other administrative staff – they're all individuals with their own personalities and their particular strengths and weaknesses, and it's just really thrilling when a new staff member starts to make big achievements using their own skills. And when you really see people develop in that way, it's just very pleasing. I like that – I like working with people.

## 2

**Interviewer** It must be difficult in your work, finding your way to a solution for industrial disputes.

**Bill** When there's a conflict between the union and an employer over some issue, I try to work it out by thinking about the different parts of the issue and setting up what I call a 'package deal'. If I can find out what the specific reasons are behind an employer's position, I can then think about ways to satisfy the employer's critical need, and protect our own interests as workers.

**Interviewer** And what does that involve?

**Bill** Well, I try to identify and understand the actual needs of the business, as well as the issues for the workers. I try to set up a package of things that I can trade on with the employer, so I can try to satisfy at least some of the employer's needs in exchange for the things that are important to us. I know this sounds logical enough, but people often put up barriers out of mistrust and don't like to change their minds on established thinking and look at issues differently. I really like it when I deal with management who are prepared to look at different solutions that may be proposed by their workers or are prepared to understand the needs of others. As a unionist, I try to do the same thing.

**Interviewer** I see. Can you give me an example of how that worked in practice?

**Bill** OK. Once we saved an important condition of employment. In bargaining for a collective agreement, an engineering company wanted to remove all overtime pay. The workers refused to give up this because it was important to them, but the employer wouldn't listen, so we were in conflict. It was important for the union to find out why the employer wanted this change so badly. We found out that this employer had recently failed to get two contracts in a very specialized area of work, because the contract was given to a lower-priced competitor. When I started negotiating with him, this employer wanted to cut costs in order to be able to compete with this specific company and win some of this work. With this understanding, we were able to make an offer to the employer that met his needs. We kept our overtime pay for general work, but we agreed that the employer could quote for this specific type of specialized work, against this specific competing company, on the basis of no extra overtime pay. We put a time limit of one year on this arrangement. One year later we extended this arrangement, but within two years the employer had won enough work to prove that his company provided better quality. And we then returned to full overtime pay.

## 3

**Interviewer** Great. Can you think of one where the workers helped solve a problem?

**Bill** I can. There was one where we and the workers saved some jobs. OK, this company manufactured telephones. The completed telephones were packaged in clear plastic bags with some information and the company brand printed on the plastic bag. They were then put into a cardboard box with the company logo printed on the box. A leaflet with manufacturer information was enclosed in the box separately. The employer announced that they were laying off three workers. We refused to cooperate with these job losses, but we had to come up with an alternative. We discovered that Head Office was demanding that local management reduce costs and that this was the reason for the lay-offs. The workers came up with an idea. Instead of duplicating the packaging, the workers came up with the idea that the phones be packed in the plastic bag only – with all of the information and the logo printed on the bag. There was no need for the cardboard box or the separate information leaflet. The extra cost of separate packaging, printing and handling was removed. As a result of this idea, and related actions there was a 5% saving in costs and the job lay-offs were cancelled. Management were so happy that they agreed to set up a regular process for workers and management to consult on better productivity.

**Interviewer** Thank you very much.

**Bill** Thank you. Any time.